This book is a must-read for mom: big 'YES' within me as I turned its of embracing our hunger for beauty an exquisite life in God—right in th. _____ of raising children, young and old—is unique. It will invite any reader to consider extravagant motherhood, where God is big and beauty can be felt even among the dishes and diapers and laundry."

SARA HAGERTY
Author of *Every Bitter Thing Is Sweet*

I suppose I have always struggled with the gap between my wildest longings for life and the often mundane details of what my days actually look like. Many times I've found myself dreaming instead of experiencing; hoping instead of embracing. Exquisite and vulnerable, Sarah Mae's writing will inspire you to bridge the gap once and for all—finding exactly what you hoped you would in a place you may have given up looking. As you read her stories, you will find yourself nodding along, grateful for a voice that understands and ultimately leads you to the peace you've been chasing.

ANGIE SMITH
Bestselling author of *Mended, I Will Carry You, What Women Fear*, and the Bible study *Seamless*

Sarah Mae has a rare gift to unearth the longings each of us feels for the "more" in life that God created us to have. Compassionate, sympathetic, and inspiring are the ways she understands our personal needs and gently leads us to the One who satisfies. This book is a gift to all who have dreamed of places beyond our present reality and want to know the hope we can cling to each day. I was deeply touched by her words.

SALLY CLARKSON
Author of *Own Your Life* and cofounder of Whole Heart Ministries

Are you struggling to figure out how to love the life you have right here and now? *Longing for Paris* shares Sarah Mae's journey to find joy and adventure in her own home and backyard. You'll be inspired to slow down, savor life, and embrace the everyday.

CRYSTAL PAINE
Founder of MoneySavingMom.com and *New York Times* bestselling author of *Say Goodbye to Survival Mode*

I love how Sarah Mae has spoken up for women's longings. She's penned the truth about how we dream and feel helpless about it when our lives demand attention to the daily. I feel seen in the pages of this book. I feel connected to my sisters. Most of all, I feel encouraged to love the space in which I live and find adventure in what already surrounds me. The things I read in *Longing for Paris* tell me I don't have to wait to really live, and that's some of the best news I have ever heard.

LISA WHITTLE
Author of *{W}hole* and *I Want God*

This book will speak to the heart of any woman who has wondered how she can fit her life-sized dreams into the tiny minutes of her every day. Through the lens of her own personal adventures, Sarah Mae frames truth with practicality and faith with tips for everyday application. In a word—*real*—Sarah Mae keeps it real. As she shares her pilgrimage to living a beautiful life, Sarah Mae's honesty is refreshing, and her message offers freedom and hope to those who read her words.

CHRYSTAL EVANS HURST
Coauthor of *Kingdom Woman*

Sarah Mae is an author who knows the deep longings of women and isn't afraid to go there. She did it with *Desperate*, and she's done it again with *Longing for Paris*. She inspires us with her relatable tales of adventure and leaves us feeling hopeful. Many of us know to "bloom where we are planted," but few of us have the courage to do it.

COURTNEY DEFEO
Author of *In This House, We Will Giggle* and founder of Lil Light O' Mine

Travel the world and change your life, or stay at home and do the same. Sarah Mae shows you the way. In *Longing for Paris*, you'll be entertained and inspired to lead a life you'll love.

CLAIRE DIAZ-ORTIZ
Author and Silicon Valley innovator

God made us to live with longing, but how do we reconcile that in our daily lives? In these pages, we get to walk with Sarah Mae to figure it out for ourselves. We find a safe place alongside this friend in searching to understand our souls and a kindred spirit who shares our sense of longing and adventuring and trying to find exactly what we've been looking for all along.

LOGAN WOLFRAM
Author, speaker, and host of the Allume conference

Our hearts and souls have become weary living in such a fast-paced world. *Longing for Paris* speaks into the desire to slow down . . . and live well right where we are. Though most of us won't be able to visit Paris, that doesn't mean we can't cultivate "Paris" in our lives. Sarah Mae shares powerful reminders to live with intentionality, savor the precious time we have with loved ones, and embrace life . . . living like the French and savoring life right down to the very last morsel!

ANGELA PERRITT
Coauthor of *You Are Loved Bible Study*, founder of LoveGodGreatly.com

Longing for Paris is one of those game-changing books. Sarah Mae leads you to a place that she herself has been . . . a place of embracing the season that you're in while holding on with hope and expectation for what is to come. Every page is filled with great truth, a depth of insight, and personal stories that will encourage and strengthen you in your own journey.

KARINA ALLEN
Blogger at *(in)courage* and *For His Name and His Renown*

Through tangles, adventures, stories, and faith, Sarah Mae's wisdom and insight is life-breath for your journey. Profound yet practical, *Longing for Paris* inspires the heart, encourages the soul, and unveils the very essence of the spirit: beauty that lies within.

LORI CORBY WOLFE
Rise Up event coordinator

Longing for Paris

Longing for PARIS

ONE WOMAN'S SEARCH
FOR JOY, BEAUTY, AND ADVENTURE—
RIGHT WHERE SHE IS

SARAH MAE

**TYNDALE®
MOMENTUM**

*An Imprint of
Tyndale House Publishers, Inc.*

Visit Tyndale online at www.tyndale.com.

Visit Tyndale Momentum online at www.tyndalemomentum.com.

Tyndale Momentum and the Tyndale Momentum logo are registered trademarks of Tyndale House Publishers, Inc., Carol Stream, IL 60188. Tyndale Momentum is an imprint of Tyndale House Publishers, Inc.

Longing for Paris: One Woman's Search for Joy, Beauty, and Adventure—Right Where She Is

Copyright © 2015 by Sarah Mae. All rights reserved.

Author Photo by Jeremy Hess Photographers, copyright © 2014. All rights reserved.

Cover illustration of Eiffel Tower copyright © Gstudio Group/Dollar Photo Club. All rights reserved.

Cover photograph of crayons and drawing copyright © Kenishirotie/Dollar Photo Club. All rights reserved.

Cover photograph of cereal copyright © mayakova/Dollar Photo Club. All rights reserved.

Cover photograph of croissant copyright © Marc Wuchner/Corbis. All rights reserved.

Cover font by Laura Worthington/Creative Market. All rights reserved.

Cover postcards "Portrait of Elisabeth of Austria, Queen of France," "Portrait of Helene Fourment, second wife of Rubens, and her children," and "The Water Mill" from Musée du Louvre and are part of the author's personal collection.

Designed by Jennifer Ghionzoli

Published in association with the literary agency of The Fedd Agency, doing business at P.O. Box 341973, Austin, TX, 78734.

Unless otherwise indicated, all Scripture quotations are taken from the New American Standard Bible,® copyright © 1960, 1962, 1963, 1968, 1971, 1972, 1973, 1975, 1977, 1995 by The Lockman Foundation. Used by permission.

Scripture quotations marked ESV are taken from *The Holy Bible*, English Standard Version® (ESV®), copyright © 2001 by Crossway, a publishing ministry of Good News Publishers. Used by permission. All rights reserved.

Scripture quotations marked NIV are taken from the Holy Bible, *New International Version,*® NIV.® Copyright © 1973, 1978, 1984, 2011 by Biblica, Inc.® Used by permission. All rights reserved worldwide.

Scripture quotations marked NLT are taken from the *Holy Bible*, New Living Translation, copyright © 1996, 2004, 2007, 2013 by Tyndale House Foundation. Used by permission of Tyndale House Publishers, Inc., Carol Stream, Illinois 60188. All rights reserved.

The Scripture quotation marked KJV is taken from the *Holy Bible*, King James Version.

Some names have been changed for the privacy of the individuals involved.

Library of Congress Cataloging-in-Publication Data

Mae, Sarah, date.
  Longing for Paris : one woman's search for joy, beauty, and adventure—right where she is / Sarah Mae.
    pages cm
  Includes bibliographical references.
  ISBN 978-1-4143-7261-7 (sc)
  1. Mae, Sarah, date. 2. Christian biography. 3. Desire—Religious aspects—Christianity. 4. Christian women—Religious life. I. Title.
  BR1725.M2155A3 2015
  277.3'083092—dc23
  [B]   2015011966

Printed in the United States of America

21	20	19	18	17	16	15
7	6	5	4	3	2	1

FOR JESSE

CONTENTS

FOREWORD

I've hiked the rugged trails of Thailand, and I've sat in awe of the Garden of Gethsemane. I've lost everything I owned in a hurricane and gone through the pain of burying my mom. Adventure and longings can fill us with lasting joy, while pain can leave us rolled into a heavy, protective shell. Now, as a mom with five young children, sometimes it's hard to give too much thought to my longings. It's hard because they all seem far-fetched. My reality is busy and demanding, and it doesn't lend itself to adventure—or so I thought. In recent years, to avoid disappointment, I chose to settle for a dull safety. Not dreaming, not longing, because I didn't want to come up empty. I compromised with my wild side, saying, "One day . . ." I allowed my flame to smolder.

Sometimes we meet a person who is never to be forgotten; Sarah Mae is one of those people. Within days of meeting her, a dream I had tucked away years ago began to rekindle. She has a way of reigniting a burnt-out wick.

As we spend time together, I can feel my courage rise, and

I catch hold of her fresh excitement for this life. As a friend, she has taught me to listen to others' hearts. She says that we are all "bursting with hidden beauty," and she desires to see that beauty unlocked. One of the ways she brings this forth is through her words of wisdom.

Her words overflow from the rich life she lives. She softly whispers correction in the ear of her energetic boy, she takes the time to curl her daughter's hair for a birthday party, and she can laugh with her husband, that sparkle still in her eye. She opens her heart and eloquently shares some of her razor-sharp experiences. She does this with such tender grace that the stories become a soothing salve for the hurting heart.

In the pages of this book, she invites us on her journey. The more I read, the more I begin to sense my own stirring. She shows us that there is, indeed, finding in the seeking. In a sense, this book is a journey back to our own awakening.

Sarah teaches us that we don't have to just press through difficult seasons in our lives. We don't have to just cope through the pain and survive. She shows us how to "untangle the tension" between longings and realities. She shakes us out of our "contentment with discontentment." She spurs our hearts to risk faith because, as she says, "When we believe God is with us, the unknown is exciting." She extends the challenge that we can wait for the right line of circumstances, or we can choose to look for fullness here in our now. With her words, she illustrates that beauty in this life is not only here, but it is here boldly beckoning.

Using the "colors of her soul," she paints a picture for us, and it's beautiful. It's vulnerable. How has she gone from the paralyzing fear of boarding an airplane to now longing for Paris—wanting to fly high over the open seas? Her journey gives freedom not just for herself, but for all of us who have longings, even longings that may be tucked away awaiting their unfolding.

I may not long for Europe the same way Sarah does, but I do long for joy. I long for beauty and art and color in my life. I want romance in the daily grind with my husband. And dare I say I long for the adventure I once lived. Like Sarah, I can't go travel the globe in search of it; so how do I find it in my everyday routine? With depth, Sarah paves the way for us. In reading this book, we are emboldened to look into our souls, listen to their stirrings, and open our hearts to the beauty that truly does exist in our realities.

Amy Smoker
Mother of five, speaker,
and cohost of A Night to Breathe
AmySmoker.com

AUTHOR'S NOTE

*Dare we awaken our hearts to their true
desires? Dare we come alive?*
JOHN ELDREDGE

I HAVE READ about women taking off to travel the world in order to discover themselves.

They journey to beautiful places and they meet interesting people, try irresistible food, and gain perspective into their souls. I have often thought about how much I would love to do that. I would love to go somewhere beautiful and release myself to it. I would love to go to Paris. But I have a family and a life that calls me to the normal everyday lifestyle, so I need to figure things out in my soul right where I am.

Some of you might relate.

Some of you might feel suffocated and are just about dying to get away or figure out your life or do something that gives breath to your soul.

I get it.

And so I'm asking, how do I navigate the tensions between my longings and my reality? How do I figure out how to enjoy my life right in the middle of the normalcy of it all?

When I began the journey nearly two years ago that has

now become this book, I was in a place where I felt stuck and tired and discouraged. Life was rolling over me, and it seemed as though I were just along for the ride. My days were controlling me instead of the other way around. But as frustrated as I was, I couldn't seem to discipline myself to make good choices.

I distinctly remember waking up one morning and thinking, *I wonder if I'll ever change. I wonder if I'll get through these years at home with my kids and realize that this season has been like water slipping through my fingers—essential to my life but beyond my ability to contain.* I wished I could hit a pause button to catch up. I didn't want to miss out on my days because I didn't want to miss out on my life. I wanted to *live wide awake*, and above all, I didn't want to regret my choices.

After having children, and coming out of the fog of sleepless nights and hormones, I realized that I was me—and yet I was different; I had to figure out who I was after having children. *I needed to discover myself again.*

That day was an awakening for me because it was then that I decided that I would no longer let the days carry me, but that I would *choose* to live.

I spent the next six months doing things like getting up early, trying new diets, parenting more intentionally, looking to do good works, and attempting to figure out who I really was. I was trying to figure out how to live an unregrettable life (the original title to this book), a life where I would be happy with the choices I made.

The initial writing of this book and the experiments I tried were the nudge to get me to wake up.

But just as I have shifted and grown a little bit more into myself, so has this book. Because I did wake up. *Here I am! I'm alive, and I want to be in it. I don't want to miss it!* Once I woke up, I began to wrestle with new feelings. I discovered that there were pieces of my soul I had hidden away, parts of me that I had decided years ago to snuff out in order to live right. And those pieces, those parts of me that God wove together, were not content to stay buried. They wanted out; they wanted to breathe and be resurrected from the dead.

No, they wouldn't stay underground.

Thumping on my soul, these longings for beauty and art and adventure wanted to be seen; I couldn't ignore them. But I didn't know what to do with them. Were they just selfish things trying to make a comeback into my life, or were they justified in wanting to be acknowledged?

I could push the longings away, but it was clear they weren't going to heed my instruction. I realized that this book was just going to have to come along for the ride as I figured out what to do with these longings in my soul.

So I began to gently peek at them in order to discern if they were real or just something I was going through—a phase that would pass. Nope, not a phase. I asked the Lord about them, and I discovered that there was a yearning in me that wanted something more, something I couldn't quite place. But on the surface, it looked like a desire to explore more of life. I was desperate to see and experience new things.

I wanted to get out of the dailiness of life and into an adventure. I wanted to travel and see and touch and do, but my life didn't afford me that luxury. I couldn't just up and leave my family in order to figure out what was going on in my soul.

On the outside, I wanted Paris. But on the inside, what I was really searching for was a filling to the deepest parts of my soul. And I wanted to know what to do with Paris and my soul and my every day.

I wanted to know how to navigate the tensions between my longings and my reality.

And I wanted to know what was behind my feelings. Could I enjoy my life and my reality right where I was, even with these longings pushing on my heart?

Yes, I want Paris, the real Paris and all the exciting things that Paris represents. But at the end of the day, I have discovered that these desires are pointing to something else.

Now is probably a good time to tell you this book isn't really about Paris.

Oh yes, we will talk about Paris, because longing for the real Paris was one of the things that woke me up and helped me get out of the mundanity of my life. But Paris really is the catalyst that got me thinking more about my longings and the deeper parts behind them.

This book is the story of me untangling my life and figuring out how to experience and enjoy the good things all around me. It's me doing something about the fact that a half-dead life is no life at all.

I know I'm not the only one who struggles with longings and the desire to understand them and do something with them. I'm not the only one who doesn't want to live like a zombie.

I believe we need each other if we are going to keep on. Life is hard enough; we shouldn't attempt to survive on our own. We need each other and to hear each other's stories to know that there is hope and that our being alive and awake to life matters. It's what the world needs.

So this book is me allowing you to watch my evolution, to come into my unfolding story, on the chance that your soul has some longings and questions and color that want to come out as well.

Thank you for coming along. It's so much better doing this together.

THE CATALYST:
Paris & Questions

(A Must-Read Introduction to Understand Le Book)

PARIS HAS FASCINATED me since I was a young girl.

Growing up, most of my life I lived with my dad and step-mom, except when I spent summers with my mom. I would lie in bed with her on those summer nights, all cozied up under soft blankets, and she would teach me French words and phrases. They all sounded so beautiful to me. With her large looping handwriting, she would scribble French words into a red notebook that had a French poodle on the cover, and I took it all in, making sure to tuck Paris into my heart. I wanted to learn, I wanted to keep listening to the beauty, and I wanted to hang on to my mom for a little bit longer because I knew the summer days would end soon enough.

My mom and her parents had lived on the outskirts of Paris when her father was stationed at the US European Command headquarters in Camp-de-Loges from 1964–1966. From the ages of ten to twelve, Mom called Maisons-Laffitte home. She told me she loved it there and that the people seemed so free, unencumbered by what others thought. They just lived and enjoyed life and food and conversation. My grandfather was also fond of Paris, particularly the wine and the eight- to eleven-course meals. Both my mother and my grandfather shared a love of the culture.

Hearing the stories of Paris from my mother and grandfather sets my heart yearning to see it for myself; I have never been there. I want to experience the beauty and the art and the food and the culture.

But this longing for Paris sparks something else in me. I find myself beginning to dream about living another life.

My imagination takes me to Paris in the 1920s. *Midnight in Paris*, one of my favorite movies, captures perfectly my ideal Paris. The movie takes the lead character, Gil Pender (played by Owen Wilson), back in time to that era, where he meets F. Scott Fitzgerald and Ernest Hemingway among other writers and artists who have a genuine camaraderie with each other in that city that seems to never lose its sparkle. I would have loved being part of that time, going to cafés every day, writing, staying up late, and having long conversations into the night about God and faith and art and music and all of the things that set flame to my soul.

My imagination takes a turn, and before long I'm dreaming of two lives, paralleling each other. In one life, I'm doing what I'm doing now. I'm married, raising my precious children, homeschooling, and, as Barbara Mouser says in *Five Aspects of Woman*, trying to raise life above the mere existence where God has me. In my other life, I move to Paris and get a place at 39 rue Descartes where Hemingway wrote, wake slowly in the mornings, ease my way into my coffee, and run my fingers on notebook pages ready to be filled. I have time to write words that matter, that encourage the soul, because I have time for depth. At the end of the day, I put my work in my bag and walk in the rain along the Seine, then stay up late in rooms filled with music and laughter. Conversations run deep, and my soul's need for beauty and purpose and relationship is realized.

Something in me aches as I come back to reality. Why these dreams? Why this longing? I'm happy with my life, thankful for all I have. *And yet . . .*

It is this longing for Paris that leads me to explore my *deeper* longings. And as I begin to look inside my soul, I see that attached to my longings are questions. Lots of questions.

"Lord," I groan, "what are these longings in my soul? Are they selfish? How do I live and sacrifice and raise my kids well and still 'follow my dreams'? Is following my dreams even biblical? What does it all mean? How do I navigate between my reality and my longings? Do I ignore them in order to sacrifice for my family? As a woman, I feel particularly confused with my longings. . . . What do I do with them?"

I want to know how to live between this tension of following my dreams and living a Jesus-following, cross-centered life. I want to know how not to shut out my longings, while at the same time giving myself to the daily work of raising my children well and not being so divided that I neglect them. I want to know, does the Lord approve of my dreams? And really, what are dreams? What are my longings, and why are they there? Can I be a good mom, an intentional mom, and also allow my longings to come to life? And can I truly enjoy my life right where I am?

It is these questions that open wide a flood of yearning in me that has been dammed up for quite a while.

And it is these questions that have led me to write this book.

Before I could begin to really enjoy my life, tasting and seeing the goodness of the Lord, I needed to sort out some of the tangles and questions in my soul (as you read above). I needed to know how God viewed me, and I needed to *see* Him. The first chapter of this book is about that untangling. Once I began to work through the mess, I started to move forward in delighting in the people and the world around me. One of the ways I found myself being more alert to the gifts around me was to find ways to bring "Paris" into my everyday life. I think you'll enjoy that fun little twist, and I hope you will join me in the sorting and then in the journey.

The unfolding journey is part serious and comes with depth and resolve, and part fun, where I am learning to enjoy the beauty and delight around me. You will read of me figuring out how to do adventure and romance, but you will also read some hard stories, stories that have shaped who I am and how they impact this whole thing, this life. Life is like that, a mix of fun and hard, beautiful and ugly, painful and life-giving. This book—the stories in it, the teaching—is all a mix, because I'm a mix of this life, as are you. I pray that the words in these pages will bring you relief where you are thirsty and a hand to hold and uplift you where you are weary.

We do not walk alone.

UNTANGLING MY SOUL

BEFORE MY HEART would even allow me to consider Paris or other dreams, I had to sort through some bitter roots, weeds that had entangled my heart. Because of my wounds and anger and sin, I had a warped view of God, one that led me to believe that He didn't really want me to enjoy the longings in my heart. I believed that God was all practicality. He was interested in me "carrying my cross," not dreaming about the stirrings in my soul. After all, I thought my longings were selfish. I needed to buck up and be responsible. Being selfless meant having no self, no color, no joy other than the fact that I was to have eternal life. In reality I had to learn to see that because I am made in the image of God, I have emotions that run deeply, long deeply, and ache deeply. I am a person of the deep.

Deep calls to deep . . .

PSALM 42:7

And because He loves me so, and because of His kindness, He led me to repentance and to clarity.

Come into my questions and see His hand as He leads me.

✺

The Bible lay on my lap, open to 2 Samuel 3. I was reading a heartbreaking scene from the story of Michal (Me-call), King David's first wife.

But first, let me give you some of her backstory. We are first introduced to Michal, the daughter of King Saul, in 1 Samuel 18:20. At the time, David was Saul's military commander—a strong and brave and handsome leader—and Michal fell in love with him. Saul, who knew that his reign was in jeopardy because of David, capitalized on his daughter's love for the future king by giving David a dangerous task to win her hand—killing one hundred Philistines. It was a mission that should have sent David to the grave, but instead sent him into the arms of the woman in waiting when he returned victorious. He had doubled what Saul had required, killing two hundred Philistines.

After Michal and David were married, Saul's jealousy got

the best of him, so he sent men to David's house to arrest him. Michal found out about the plot and helped David escape. When she knew he was safe, she covered for her husband, by stalling and filling his bed with items that made it look like David was there. Of course, Saul's henchmen discovered the ruse, and soon after, Saul began a relentless manhunt for David (see 1 Samuel 19:11-17).

While David was on the run, he took at least two more wives. Saul had given Michal to another man—Palti—to marry.

David continued to assert his power and build up loyalty, and right before he became king, he demanded Michal's return. She was torn from Palti, who wept as she left and followed her, powerless to stop what was happening. Finally David's men told him to go home (2 Samuel 3:16).

Michal, the woman who had once loved David, now "despised him in her heart" (2 Samuel 6:16). Her reaction could have been the result of feeling neglected while David was fighting, being jealous of David's success as king, loathing him for taking other wives, or having second thoughts about her loyalty to him instead of her father. Venom spewed from her mouth when she saw King David celebrating the return of the Ark of God, the first time she had seen him since that night she helped him escape years before. Her words were meant to shame him.

How could her heart that had burned with such love for this man now be filled with such disdain? David basically tells her off, and the last we hear of Michal are these fateful words: She "had no child to the day of her death" (2 Samuel 6:23).

And that's it. That's all we know.

My heart ached for Michal, for this woman who seemed to be a pawn between her father and her husband and power. And my ache led to questions, as pain oftentimes does, and then it made me mad, so I gave God my questions. "God, did You even care about Michal's heart? Do You even care about women? *Do You even care about me?*"

I needed to know how God saw me. I needed to know I was more than parts, more than a pawn, more than a cursed woman trying to figure out how to live redeemed in a fallen world where men hurt women.

I needed to know what it meant for me, as a woman, to have a calling or a dream or longings. This was personal, not only for me, but for my daughters.

WHO AM I, GOD?

How could I possibly begin to understand my longings if I didn't even understand who I was to God? How could I begin to truly enjoy my life if I had these deep-seated questions?

I have been a Christian for many years now, and I know Jesus and His grace and His love. I have had great training in the Scriptures and in discipleship through The Navigators ministry. I have been poured into and have pored over the Scriptures for years, leading Bible studies and giving talks to encourage women in faith. And yet there I was, *begging* God to tell me how He viewed me. I was desperate to know what I meant to Him as a woman.

I ended up in the book of Job. I have read Job before, and I wasn't interested in reading it again. Yet I felt led to read it again.

I read and I pondered, and I saw that Job accused God, just as I had.

Everything had been taken away from Job—his family, wealth, possessions, even his health. He was suffering in pain and yet trying to hold on to his integrity and righteousness before the Lord. But it was getting to be too much to bear.

I have pulled just a few lines from his bold accusations aimed at God.

> *Is not man forced to labor on earth, and are not his days like the days of a hired man?* (7:1); *You destroy man's hope. You forever overpower him and he departs.* (14:19-20); . . . *God has wronged me.* (19:6); . . . *Why should I not be impatient? . . . Why do the wicked still live, continue on, [and] also become very powerful?* (21:4,7); *Oh that I knew where I might find Him, that I might come to His seat! I would present my case before Him and fill my mouth with arguments.* (23:3-4); . . . *You have become cruel to me.* (30:21)

Job throws questions and indictments at God, exactly like I did: "Why, God? You are unjust! I don't even know if You're really good."

But then along comes Elihu, a young man who has remained quiet while Job's other three friends' counsel exasperates Job and angers God.

Finally, Elihu can't hold it in any longer or he'll burst. He says,

> *I am young in years and you are old; therefore I was*
> *shy and afraid to tell you what I think. I thought age*
> *should speak, and increased years should teach wisdom.*
> *But it is a spirit in man, and the breath of the Almighty*
> *gives them understanding.*
> JOB 32:6-8

After Elihu puts the three older friends in their place, he goes through the list of reasons Job has given for feeling he's been shortchanged by God and deserves answers. Elihu says, "Let me tell you, you are not right in this" (33:12).

> *Far be it from God to do wickedness.* (34:10)
> *One who is perfect in knowledge is with you.* (36:4)
> *Whether for correction, or for His world, or for*
> *lovingkindness, He causes it to happen.* (37:13)

And then, God says to Job . . .

> *Gird up your loins like a man, and I will ask you, and*
> *you instruct Me!*
> JOB 38:3

Job finally has an audience with God. And it's God's turn to barrage Job with questions, ones that none of us can even begin to fathom.

> *Where were you when I laid the foundation of the earth? Tell Me, if you have understanding, who set its measurements? Since you know. Or who stretched the line on it? On what were its bases sunk? Or who laid its cornerstone, when the morning stars sang together and all the sons of God shouted for joy?*
>
> JOB 38:4-7

God speaks two chapters' worth to Job, and in all of it He's asking Job to see Him for who He is. He is the almighty God, and all that exists is under His authority. He has reasons for His plans, reasons we cannot even begin to comprehend with our finite minds that hold such limited knowledge.

You know what Job says in return?

> *I have declared that which I did not understand.* . . . *I have heard of You by the hearing of the ear;* but now my eye sees You; *therefore I retract, and I repent in dust and ashes.*
>
> JOB 42:3, 5-6 (EMPHASIS ADDED)

Job wasn't repenting because he *did* something; he was repenting because he *didn't see God for who He is*, and he *didn't see God's love* for him. Job felt like a hired hand, and quite frankly, he was prideful. He recognized God's power, but he thought he had God's understanding.

As I read through and pondered Job's lament, considered Elihu's rebuke, and paid attention to God's rebuttal, I began to *see* Him.

In Hosea 2:16-20 (NIV), the Lord says, "In that day you will call me 'my husband.' . . . I will betroth you to me forever; I will betroth you in righteousness and justice, in love and compassion. I will betroth you in faithfulness, and you will acknowledge the LORD."

Oh, that I would see Him and know Him!

THE COMMUNION TABLE

I found myself in the middle of all my accusations and confusion, and with thoughts of Job and Hosea swirling in my head, at a Sunday Communion service. Sitting in my chair, I took the bread and the wine, and in that moment the Lord spoke to my heart. All of a sudden, the truth was clear as day: *God didn't die for a woman; He died for me, because He loves me and I'm worth His very life for me to see Him.* God died for His *loves*. He wasn't obligated to die; He chose to. And now, I'm His *daughter*.

I see You, God. I see You.

I could stop asking, "Why God?" and start saying, "Teach me to see what I do not see."

It's interesting that God uses the Communion table to

make us see Him. In fact, after Jesus' resurrection, His own disciples didn't recognize Him until He broke bread with them:

> *When He had reclined at the table with them, He took the bread and blessed it, and breaking it, He began giving it to them. Then their eyes were opened and they recognized Him.*
>
> LUKE 24:30-31

We see Him in the sacrifice. We see His love for us and His great mercy when we see that He was broken for us. He was broken for you and for me, personally.

I wished that Michal had been sitting beside me at that moment. There is so much that Scripture doesn't tell us, hidden things in her story, things I wished I could ask her and then share with her about God. I know this for certain: God cares about women, and He cared about Michal. I know this because He hasn't changed; His character is the same yesterday, today, and forever. If He cared and died for me, I can tell you He cared for Michal and He loved her.

God sees us, but how often do we truly see Him? He wants us to see that there is not one unjust or wicked thing in Him. He is fully good, and He is fully *for us.*

Let's face it. When we're hurt, we put up walls. We want to know, "Can I trust You, God?"

We're afraid we can't trust Him. Why?

Because we're afraid He won't come through.

And, yet, as we begin to see Him for who He is, we see He is trustworthy. He helps us see ourselves for who we are.

I can't speak to the specific strongholds that might be in your life, but I can say this: If you're at that point where you are desperate to hear Him like I was, then you are blessed.

"Blessed are the poor in spirit" (Matthew 5:3). The literal meaning of that Scripture is "blessed are those as helpless as a beggar."

You are in a good place. God wants to bring you to where you can see Him and know who you are. Your destiny is not to be in pain, but to walk in confidence and know who you are as His son or daughter.

> *The LORD your God is in your midst, a victorious warrior. He will exult over you with joy, He will be quiet in His love, He will rejoice over you with shouts of joy.*
>
> ZEPHANIAH 3:17

> *As the bridegroom rejoices over the bride, so your God will rejoice over you.*
>
> ISAIAH 62:5

As I began to see myself as a beloved daughter of the God who is not only my Father, but a happy Father who smiles over me, I began to see my longings in a new light.

GOD CARES ABOUT OUR DREAMS

She told me that God cares about our dreams.

Her words made me catch my breath.

There we were, the three of us, friends huddled close at a restaurant talking over chips and dip and the most delicious chocolate cake. And she said those words: God cares about our dreams.

He does? I had thought that dreams were selfish, mostly, and the thought that He cared about dreams *never even entered my mind.* I remember another friend telling me once that she didn't even think dreams, as in "following our dreams," was even a biblical concept.

I was so confused. But this conversation at the restaurant did something to me; I felt the truth of my friend's words in my spirit as soon as they were uttered. And I was changed.

I knew in my depths that what she said was true: God cares about our dreams, because He cares about us.

He cares about me, His daughter, whom He loves and delights in. He cares about you, too.

There it is, the first thing in figuring out how to think about our longings and dreams: Our God cares about them. This is important theology. If God cares about us and delights in us and therefore cares about the things we care about as a Father cares for the joy in His children, we can exhale.

I've been so concerned with being "right" and "good" that I never stopped to contemplate the heart of my Father and

His pleasure over the things that stir my heart. He made me for goodness sake! He knew every piece of me before He even breathed a soul into me.

And He not only knew me; He designed me. He put the very ability to long in my soul; He gave me the gift of dreaming so I could have vision in this life.

The Bible says that without vision a people perish (see Proverbs 29:18, kjv). We need our dreams to give us the motivation to have a plan so that we can keep on. With no vision and no dreams and no longings, we lack the ability to creatively and joyously make plans for how we will spend our days. Granted, the Lord directs our steps, but we faithfully begin the walking of them.

Oh yes, dreams are biblical and good, and we can thank God for them.

I have learned that where we go wrong is when we hold so tightly to our dreams that we neglect to fully trust God with them. The reality is, some dreams are woven into our souls from our Creator, and some are the result of our sinfulness. The good news is we can ascertain which dreams are good and which are of the flesh by asking ourselves some "search me" questions, and then be open to God's revelation to our hearts. I'll explain the questions in a minute.

The other trouble we run into with our dreams is when we take our very good dreams and try to walk them out before their time, which can bring frustration and/or neglect to our families or where God has us. We all need time in the pasture, so to speak, where we can mature in faithfulness.

I call these years the "hidden years." Consider David. As a young shepherd, he was hidden in the pasture tending to sheep, learning how to direct them and care for them before he would direct and care for a nation as a king. If we can be patient and trust our Father with the timing of our lives, I believe He will use us as He sees fit in His time.

But how do we deal with these longings in the meantime? What do we do with them?

Throughout this book you will see how I've been dealing with my longings, and I'll even talk more in depth about dreams and longings in chapter 7, but for now, this:

If you're anything like me, in the everyday of life, there seems to be a constant pull between self (the things I desire) and sacrifice. I want to do what I want to do, but my kids need me present and available most of the days, particularly because I have chosen to homeschool. They are my first work, so they get priority (in theory). But it is a battle. I have to choose daily to trust that God will use me when and how He pleases. I may not be able to use the gifts He's given me outside of family full-time right now, but one day I may be able to. Perhaps one day I'll be able to travel to Paris and maybe even take my family! I don't know what the future holds, but I know that the God who holds it is good.

My friend Carrie Crawford, a breast cancer survivor, says, "Not what if, but *even if.*"

Even if I never go to Paris, He is good.

Even if I never have my longings fulfilled on this earth, He is good.

Even if something terrible happens to me or my family or friends, He is good.

Is it settled in your heart that He is good?

As you'll read in chapter 9, our longings are far deeper than what we sometimes think them to be.

In the meantime, on this earth and in our reality, whatever that may be, we trust. We hold on to our dreams with open hands, and we walk out this life one day at a time believing that our God cares about our dreams.

Because, friend, He does.

> *For You formed my inward parts;*
> *You wove me in my mother's womb.*
> *I will give thanks to You, for I am fearfully and*
> *   wonderfully made;*
> *Wonderful are Your works,*
> *And my soul knows it very well.*
>
> PSALM 139:13-14

> *. . . the LORD takes pleasure in His people.*
>
> PSALM 149:4

GOD DELIGHTS IN US AND IS GLORIFIED WHEN WE DELIGHT IN HIM

Now I understand.

Because He cares for me and delights in me and wants me to delight in Him, I am free to enjoy the beauty around me.

His creation is a gift.

As I acknowledge that and thank Him for it, I unwrap more and more of His goodness and kindness.

It is like the delight I get when my children tumble out of their beds on Christmas morning, anxious to see and touch and open their gifts. Last Christmas, as I was in my bedroom, I heard them up and down the stairs all night, scurrying across the hardwood floors, back and forth between the living room and their bedroom, because they just couldn't contain their excitement. I yelled at them to get back in bed. But after I yelled, I smiled because *I knew.*

The next morning, the three of them got up early—before Jesse and me—to open and play with the one gift each that they are allowed to open without us. At 8 a.m. they jumped on our bed to get us up, and I brewed the coffee to help open our eyes to the glory of the day. Then Jesse and I settled in for the joy of watching our children open the rest of their gifts. Like past Christmases, I couldn't get enough of the brightness in their eyes, the giggles, and the utter, unabashed joy. I am delighted when they are delighted in the gifts we have chosen for them.

And it is this joy and delight that I believe God has when we enjoy His gifts.

He loves us, His daughters, and He is delighted when we delight in Him. In fact, we are told in Psalm 34:8 to "taste and see that the LORD is good."

My youngest daughter laid three books on my bed. "Will you read these to me?" she asked.

"Just one," I said. "Mommy's busy."

She looked at the books, pondered, and made her choice.

She curled up next to me and snuggled in close, her head resting on my shoulder as I read the story.

When that one was finished, she handed me the next one.

"Okay, I'll read *one* more." I did this because she was so close and so dear.

I read the third one because I'm a sucker.

After the last book was done, she closed her eyes and stayed awhile. We were cozy and warm. I smelled her hair, and I rubbed her head—and I thanked God that He had given her to me as my daughter. She is so precious. In her I *see* that the Lord is good.

Taste and see . . .

I'm going to do that; I'm going to take Him up on His offer to "taste and see that the Lord is good."

HOW CAN WE NAVIGATE THE TENSIONS BETWEEN OUR REALITY AND OUR LONGINGS?

1. We believe truth. God does care about our dreams and our longings.

2. God gives us gifts to be used for His Kingdom purposes on this earth; we have purpose here.

3. God delights in us and the pleasure we receive from His gifts in us. He is a fun and colorful God, and He is happy with us because we are His.

4. He delights when we trust Him completely, knowing He does all things for the good of those who love Him.

5. He wants us to seek His face. He wants us to commune with Him.

6. We search our hearts and see if there is any offensive way in us (see Psalm 139:24, NIV). What is the motivation behind our dreams and longings? We wrestle this out in vulnerability, knowing we will most likely have to do this several times over our lifetime.

7. We give our dreams and longings to Him, trusting Him to do as He pleases, knowing He cares about us, our growth, and our total trust in Him.

8. We walk by faith, doing what we can when we can, knowing the season we're in and the extent of our capacity.

9. We recognize our longings are in us for a deeper purpose.

✍ Unearthing Your Longings

What are you longing for, deep down in the depths of your soul? Take some time and think on it, getting to the root of your heart's desire. What fears do you have when it comes to your longings? Are you hurt, scared, angry, or sad about them? Offer your longings to the One who made you who you are. Ask Him to teach you what you do not see. Ask Him to help you to see Him for who He is: good and compassionate and a Father who cares about your dreams, a Father who *delights* in you.

Go deeper by meditating on Job 42:3-6 and Zephaniah 3:17.

AN INVITATION TO PARIS!

Use your imagination . . . go on, close your eyes and dream. What would you do if you could go to Paris (or another place that calls to your heart)? What would you want to see? Where does your imagination take you? Keep the dreams of your imagination close, as you will be revisiting them during this journey of bringing Paris to right where you are.

2

EVERYDAY ADVENTURE

LET THE PARIS ADVENTURE BEGIN.

Well, the version of Paris that is Lititz, Pennsylvania, my charming little town—home to Café Chocolate, Tomato Pie Café, and a cute little downtown area that comes alive on the first Friday of every month during the summer with music and art and food. It is here I will begin to bring some Paris into my everyday life in order to taste and see the goodness of the Lord. I want to enjoy Him, and I want to live wide awake right where He has me.

Some might be reading this and thinking, *This is silliness, just fanciful living and not really caring about the hurting or all the sin and ache in the world.* Here's what I want to say to that:

There is more at stake to this project than fanciful living, but sometimes fanciful living keeps us awake, and we need to be an alive people of God. When we are alive, we can call forth life in others, encouraging each other to keep on and "to act justly and to love mercy and to walk humbly" with our God (see Micah 6:8). A fully alive people living for the living God can accomplish much in the world, but a half-dead people will just survive.

I'm no longer willing to just survive. I'm going to live, and I'm going to follow my God, believing Him, enjoying Him, and being used by Him for Kingdom purpose.

After all, I have experienced adventure before.

❧

When I was seventeen, my best friend, Tania, and I jumped into my white Plymouth Duster and drove from State College, Pennsylvania, to Atlanta, Georgia—straight through in thirteen hours. We drove ninety miles an hour nearly the whole trip. We were reckless and young and crazy. But, oh, did we have fun. Singing at the top of our lungs, windows down, not a care in the world.

At twenty-one, I was at a Navigators retreat in Colorado over spring break and snuck out of camp with a group of friends to go climbing in the Rocky Mountains. I had never climbed anything that high before. But it was a beautiful sunny day, and that mountain was begging us to hike it. So we did.

It didn't start out too steep, but the more we climbed, the

steeper it got. We had to climb nearly straight up, holding on to each rock with our fingers and carefully positioning our sneakered feet so we wouldn't slip and fall. As the terrain became more treacherous, some of the "adventurers" decided to turn back, but not me.

Let me tell you: Colorado from the top of a mountain is a glory to behold. The four of us who made it to the summit took in the magnificent sight, proud of our exhilarating accomplishment. Of course, what goes up must come down. All I will say is that our descent was an adventure all its own.

Before we left the Rockies behind, we went to Breckenridge, where I skied on something bigger than a glorified speed bump for the first time. I felt free.

At twenty-two, I packed up my Jeep and drove to Memphis, Tennessee, to work as a lifeguard at an inner-city kids' camp for the summer. The place where I was staying was Otis Redding's former recording studio, which had been purchased and gutted for renovation by The Navigators. I was the only one living there, and because of the renovation, there was no bathroom in the house. When you had to go, you had to go out, around the pool, and over to an outhouse. Um, no. When it's dark, in a dangerous neighborhood, you do not go outside and around the pool to the bathroom. You find other ways to take care of business.

Moving along . . .

It was scary enough being there by myself and even scarier when the house was broken into with me in it! Fortunately, the intruder was spooked by my alarm and fled. After that, I stayed with the camp director and his wife, making their couch my bed. When other interns joined me later in the summer, we'd sit on the pool deck at night and hear the distant sound of gun shots ringing in the air. It was a crazy, but memorable, adventure to share together.

At twenty-three I got married, and at twenty-five I had my first baby. By twenty-nine I had three children under the age of four, was a stay-at-home mom, and was feeling desperate. Eventually the desperate feelings eased as I entered a new season of my children getting older and me getting sleep. I didn't feel desperate, but I did feel stuck.

What happened to me?

It seemed my adventuring days were over.

HOW TO GO ADVENTURING IN YOUR ORDINARY, EVERYDAY LIFE

To be clear, I have no interest in bungee jumping off a bridge, going skydiving, or snorkeling in the ocean. That is *not* my definition of adventure. I'm much too tame.

However, my longing for something more began out of one of my GET ME OUT OF HERE moments. Oh yes, I have those. I get in these funks where I become very dramatic, and I'm all, "I'm *dying*. I *have* to get out of the house. I *cannot take it* one more second."

And Jesse's like, "Oh great, here we go. We're not spending any money just because you need to get out."

Me: "But I'm going to die."

After I had repeated this lament a number of times, Jesse came up with an idea.

So on the morning of a recent Fourth of July my husband said, "Why don't we go downtown with the kids and have a scavenger hunt?"

"Scavenger hunt, hmmm . . . that sounds like quite a bit of work. Are you tricking me?"

"No, it will be simple and fun. Come on!"

I gave Jesse the side-eye, but I followed.

When we arrived downtown, Jesse gave the kids instructions. "As we explore, Mommy and I will tell you to find something or do something. The one who finds it gets a dime." *Ahhh, I get it. Not only will the kids have fun, but Jesse and I can enjoy ourselves and curb the "I wants" with a fun little game. Genius.* As we walked around, Jesse would say something like, "How many American flags can you see? How many stripes does it have? Stars?" Dime. Dime. Dime. EASY. I'm pretty sure he only spent five dollars total.

True, this trip wasn't anything wild, but it was an adventure for our family. Which makes me realize that in recent years I've had a very narrow view of adventure. I say this because I would love to go off to Paris and see and smell and taste and touch . . . oh, yes! To wander the city streets, pop into cafés here and there, talk with the locals, meander through the markets, and enjoy each day—take me, please! But that's still a dream for now. Instead, I'm searching for another kind of exploring that is more realistic, something much simpler for me to implement with my kids. A Fourth-of-July-spontaneous-on-a-dime kind of adventuring.

According to my friend Jillian, adventure is what you make it. She told me a story about her mom that has forever altered my perspective:

It was a school night marked by the general chaos of a family with three girls ranging in age from elementary school to high school. Soccer practice, band practice, college visits—it seemed like my family never stopped moving. My parents wanted the best for my younger sisters and me and did everything they could to run us around to all of our extracurricular activities and provide for us. At the end of this particular evening, each family member retreated to their respective bedrooms after dinner, settling in for a night of silence and work.

I didn't think anyone was awake when Mom knocked on my bedroom door.

"Yah," I said with a hint of seventeen-year-old attitude. It was my senior year, and college applications were piling up—I was constantly stressed and worried about my future.

"Jilly, want to take a break?"

I glanced at my piles of homework and hesitated. I didn't answer her.

She opened the door a little further, slowly.

"It's just," she offered, "it's just . . . I'm really hungry for a cheeseburger."

I looked up from my paper, surprised. She broke a smile, and I nodded, grabbing a sweatshirt as I headed out the door. My room was right down the hall from my sister's, and Mom made a dramatic effort to tiptoe past her door unheard.

When we got into the car, I sat bewildered, watching Mom adjust the driver's seat and visibly relax, as if the stresses of the real world were just a dream.

She turned the radio station to rock and roll, the volume all the way up.

"Your dad and I used to take long drives with this song—I used to roll all the windows down, and I'd let my feet hang out the window the whole way home."

The memory lit up Mom's eyes as we headed down the street, her dark eyes reflecting the oncoming headlights. She took the scenic route, talking all the way.

"I used to sing so loud the cars next to me would honk, and I'd drive faster to pass them, turning my head to look and smile."

And then she laughed.

I loved Mom's laugh, so wild and free and unashamed.

We pulled into the drive-thru lane of Burger King as she continued.

"I used to play pranks on the order taker. I'd lean real close to the speaker and just scream my order until my voice went hoarse, just for fun."

It only took a few minutes to get home with our late-night snack. We sat in the driveway. Mom propped her legs up on the dashboard next to mine, and we ate, not ready to go inside. "This will be our own little secret," she said. Our voices filled every inch of the car with story after story, and I met a mother I never realized I had. She laughed and I couldn't help but match her smile; I couldn't help but wonder if someday I would become like her.

Maybe it was minutes and maybe it was hours that we sat together—all I know is that years have gone by and I've yet to eat a more delicious meal. When I think of growing up, I always think of this moment with my mom. It was small, but it felt true. It felt like adventure.

What a relief. I don't have to traverse Mount Everest to have an adventure with my kids! If I just do *something out of the ordinary*, we can have adventures.

With Jillian's story in mind, I recently went up to my oldest daughter's bedroom. She was in bed, still awake.

"Do you want to go out and get some treats and watch a movie with me?"

She grinned big. I didn't even make her change out of her pj's. She put on a coat, and we headed to the grocery store. She picked out the biggest, most delicious looking cupcake she could find from the bakery. Then we wandered around, looking for something to fill my craving. I landed on lobster bisque. We headed home with our loot, and after I heated up my treat, we tucked ourselves into my bed for snuggles, good eats, and a movie; just the two of us. It was a sweet time, our own little adventure.

Before you begin planning your adventure with your kids, I have to forewarn you. It might be best if you come up with ideas first.

I made the mistake of asking my children what they considered to be an adventure.

Oldest daughter (age 9): "Going to Chuck E. Cheese's with just girls."

Son (age 7): "First, I'd go in the jungle, and then I would go on a lava mountain and go through it and get all the diamonds and gold, and then it would explode. Then I would go through a different forest with vines, and I'd find a pirate sword and a dead pirate with ripped clothes and gold on him worth $9,000."

"But what about an adventure with me?"

"Same thing, except that I'd share the stuff with you."

Youngest daughter (age 5): "It's when you find cool things and treasure."

"What about an adventure with me?"

"We would go in the jungle."

Huh. I'm going to have to *majorly* lower their expectations.

THE GREAT CROISSANT HUNT

I had never eaten a croissant before I began this book.

At least, not that I remember. But since the croissant is a staple in the French diet, and in order to bring some Paris to where I am, I decided to hunt down the best croissant in Lititz, Pennsylvania, bringing my kids along for the journey. I did my research, and off we went in pursuit of the perfect French pastry. Here are the places where we tried croissants:

Tomato Pie Café

Giant (grocery store)

Dosie Dough

Lititz Family Cupboard

(For those of you living in Lititz or for anyone who has visited, you may wonder why we didn't try Café Chocolate. Well, I tried. Sort of.)

My kiddos and I headed out one morning to walk around downtown Lititz, hitting up every bakery we came across in our search for the best croissant. We were on a mission. However, we were quickly dismayed to find that not only were some places closed at 8 a.m. (hello, morning coffee?), but most places do not make their own fresh croissants.

Back to Café Chocolate. We never did go there because they don't open until 10:30 a.m. I did call later to ask if they made their croissants at the restaurant, and they informed me (which by now had become the standard answer) that they "had them shipped in." Unfortunately, by the time I got around to confirming this, I had become a croissant snob who only wanted them freshly baked.

Which brings me to the winner of the great croissant hunt (and the place I most frequented throughout the summer with my kids).

The only place in Lititz where I could find fresh croissants available daily was Dosie Dough, who had them delivered from a Philadelphia bakery (only two hours away) each morning.

Not only were the croissants perfectly flaky and flavorful, but I became completely smitten with Dosie Dough—falling in love with them during our summer expedition.

When we walked inside, we were greeted with flyers to the left plastered on a community bulletin board, a cashier in front, coffee to the right (self-serve), and a large glass case featuring the day's treats. We scooted past the people in line and went around the glass case to place our orders.

"I'd like a croissant, please." The young woman pulled a croissant out and asked me, "Would you like it grilled?"

I've noticed a trend here in Lancaster County: You do not eat a croissant as is—you order it slightly grilled. I like a croissant buttered and grilled, just enough to warm it up.

"Sure," I said.

My kids picked out chocolate covered pretzel pastries, and we went to the end of the line to pay.

Dosie Dough doesn't have inside seating, but they have a wonderful patio with tables and chairs, which is the perfect place to enjoy sweet splurges on a summer morning.

Side note: Another thing I love about Dosie Dough is that they have a piano outside for anyone to play. My children love this and have a jolly time making music. The piano is painted blue and green and pink, decorated with fun illustrations of multicolored pretzels.

That morning we sat down at a table on the patio, but before I allowed the kids to dig right in or plunk on the piano keys, I gave them instructions. "Close your eyes. Take a bite, and as you chew slowly, I want you to think of how it tastes. Savor it. Now, tell me, what do you taste? Describe it to me."

This is my approach to trying new food with my family, something I began while working on this book. I want everyone to actually taste the food and enjoy the goodness of it, rather than just shove it in their mouths. After all, God made food with taste, didn't He? So taste we will!

OUT OF THE ORDINARY: *Feeding the Homeless*

Thank goodness, there is no one-size-fits-all definition for adventure. My eyes are being opened to simple, ordinary adventures all around me. I'm up for doing things out of the ordinary, but I believe they should be things that matter to my family.

Recently, we had such an opportunity—an adventure that I didn't even realize was an adventure until Jesse pointed it out. It began with a text from my friend Amy a few days before Thanksgiving. "We are going to bring hot breakfast plates into Lancaster City on Thanksgiving morning. Just gonna drive around and hand them out to the homeless. Y'all are welcome to join us."

Jesse and I didn't even have to think about it. Yes! We'd never done that before, but it was something we both wanted to be part of—a gesture of kindness to meet a real need.

Because everything was so last-minute, Amy did all the cooking. All we (my family and I) had to do was show up. At 6:30 on Thanksgiving morning we got up, got dressed, and headed over to Amy's house. When she opened the door, the aroma alone that greeted us made our mouths water. Amy had prepared twenty plates of food, with generous helpings of pancakes, omelets, bacon, and grits. (Breakfast for a Mississippi gal must include grits.) And, of course, there was a large container of coffee. Did I mention that Amy has five kids under the age of ten, and her youngest isn't even two? Yet she got up early on Thanksgiving morning and cooked all that food in order to serve those who didn't have any. I am still in awe of her selflessness.

Our husbands packed everything up in our two vehicles (including all eight kids), and we all headed to the city of Lancaster. We knew a particular place where some of the homeless gather, so we went there first and found five people. We got out of our cars, walked up to the group, and asked them if they'd like a hot breakfast and coffee. Emphatic yeses all around!

A few minutes later, more people arrived, each one of them thanking us for such a good meal. One man said he hadn't eaten in two days. Everyone we served was appreciative, and no one asked for anything else from us. When we got back in our cars, we didn't have to go very far to find others who were grateful to receive the hand-delivered meals.

As we drove home, Jesse and I talked about the adventure. "So what did you think?" he asked.

"I have to be honest," I replied. "I was kind of scared about doing this because it's way out of my comfort zone. You know me; I don't like facing the unknown. Walking up to strangers and asking them if they'd like a plate of food is a big unknown. But it turned out not to be so scary after all."

I had had a fear of feeding the homeless, but that fear has been overcome because Amy included us in an adventure of serving the community. I'll do it again without a moment's hesitation.

What new adventures await us? I don't know at the moment, but . . . bring 'em on.

MY HUSBAND'S LEAP OF FAITH

Since Jesse and I have been keeping an eye out for adventure in our lives, it shouldn't have been a surprise when God led us to one of our seemingly craziest adventures yet. But first, let me give you some background.

From the time he was a boy, Jesse had always dreamed of becoming a police officer. He carried this dream in his heart, and as he grew older he made choices that would lead to the fulfillment of his dream. He read up on the criteria for becoming a police officer—from physical fitness to mental competence—everything he needed in order to be considered for the job. He knew what he was and wasn't capable of in his life, so that when the time came to take a lie-detector test he would be able to answer honestly and pass with flying colors.

After Jesse graduated from high school, he went to Penn State University to study crime, law, and justice. In his senior year, he got a semester-long internship with a police department. When he began applying for police jobs, he was ready.

Just to note, when you apply to become a police officer, it is not just filling out an application and being called in for an interview; it is a long process that takes weeks to complete, including psychological tests, physical tests, detective interviews with family and friends, and other exams. And the competition is pretty fierce—hundreds of people apply for a few open positions.

We were newly married and with a baby on the way when Jesse went through a few of these processes. After everything was done, he was offered jobs by two different police departments. He joyfully accepted one of them. His dream was finally about to be realized.

And then a couple of days later he got a call.

"I'm sorry, Jesse, but we can't hire you. We just found out

that the police academy won't pass anyone who has hearing aids."

Yes, my husband is partially deaf in both ears. He wears state-of-the-art, in-the-ear hearing aids (that don't fall out), and hearing tests prove he can hear better than some people with normal hearing. However, because of laws passed in the seventies—pretty standard throughout the United States—before technology had vastly improved hearing aids, Jesse was unable to become a police officer.

My husband was crushed.

He had worked his whole life toward this one goal, and when it was taken from him—even though he was qualified—it broke his heart.

He became depressed. Right before my eyes, my husband changed into someone who just stopped caring.

He got very quiet, and his face became hard. Pain was turning into bitterness.

He was angry and despondent.

As his wife with our new baby, I was scared.

Jesse is a good man and wanted to provide for our family, so he took a job in another town where HVAC (heating, ventilating, and air-conditioning) installation work was available. Eventually he became a plumber/maintenance man at a school district, resigning himself to the fact that this would be his life.

He lost the ability to dream, because his lifelong dream never came to fruition.

Jesse became cynical and wary of trusting the God who

put a dream in his heart and then gave him a disability that would prevent that dream from ever coming true. Oh, we went to church together on Sundays, but his heart held back.

Now, my husband is a rock. He likes stability and safety, and he has a very strong work ethic. Even though he greatly disliked his job, he worked hard in order to take care of our family. He never even called in sick unless he was practically on his deathbed. That's my man.

For years, he endured a job he didn't like without voicing a complaint to me. But around year nine, Jesse began to have stirrings in his heart; he wanted something more out of life than the daily grind. He didn't feel content with his discontent anymore—something in his heart wanted to come alive again. What was dead was resurrecting.

I'll never forget the first time I saw it, the new life gently pushing on the soil of his heart. He said, "I think I'd like to find a way to do something else, and maybe not stay at my job my whole life."

That was huge. I remember looking at him with shock and saying, "Whoa, whoa, whoa. What?"

He had always told me that he would never leave his job. He would retire there so we could be secure. And now this.

I was thrilled because it meant he was letting himself be tender to the possibilities of the future. It also meant he was willing to let faith breathe again.

We prayed and cried and prayed and begged God to show us what this all meant. My husband was no longer the man who was going to just "stay in this job forever because it's stable." God was preparing us for something new.

A new desire began to grow in my husband's heart. He began to draw and to envision creating things out of reclaimed wood. He has always loved working with his hands and he has an artist's heart, but he was never sure what to do with it. He began to tinker with making wall hangings and furniture out of wood he would find on the side of the road. People began to encourage him in his work; he was making beautiful objects. And he loved it.

Through a series of events that unfolded over a year's time, my husband did something I thought I would never see him do.

My husband, the rock, Mr. Stability, took a crazy risk by faith, and quit his job.

I am so proud of him. Our family is experiencing one big adventure each and every day as we see how God is guiding us into a deeper trust of Him, while bringing Jesse's dream to fruition. It's magical to watch.

I don't know how this adventure will play out, but I can tell you that it's exhilarating and scary and good all at the same time.

THE MOST EXCITING ADVENTURE

The wind blows where it wishes and you hear the sound of it, but do not know where it comes from and where it is going; so is everyone who is born of the Spirit.
JOHN 3:8

In the Gospel of John, Jesus describes the Holy Spirit as being like the wind—we don't know where the Holy Spirit is going or where it comes from.

I think one of the greatest adventures for those of us who put our trust in the Lord is allowing the Holy Spirit to lead us, even when we have no idea where that might be. Yes, there can be fear in the unknown, but when we face our fears and choose to hand them to God, who says, "Do not fear, for I am with you" (Isaiah 41:10), not only can we overcome our fears but we can look at the unknown with a new perspective, a sense of adventure. When we believe God is with us, the unknown is exciting; He doesn't leave us, and He cares about our future. And this message, this truth of following by faith in trust, isn't just for people who are living good lives; it's for all of us. No matter the circumstance, God's loving-kindness is with us. It's not a trite thing. There isn't a person on this earth He doesn't want to see come to know Him and experience His love and freedom.

No one is forgotten. He cares for broken people and the brokenhearted and often uses us to show that care—to hungry homeless people and a husband with a dream. I want to be a part of the adventure that follows by faith in bringing God's Kingdom to bear, setting captives free, and seeing sons and daughters claim their inheritance of who they are. Freedom comes with total trust in the One who holds our souls and calls us His children.

By faith we keep on.

Our adventure in faith meets up with other people's

adventures in faith, and God's glory is revealed, showing that there is hope and that lives can be restored. This is real adventure.

So yes, there's Paris, and I want Paris. But I have faith in the God who made Paris and made hearts long to be alive with goodness.

We are a part of an unfolding story that is filled with adventure. Count me in.

✐ *Unearthing Your Longings*

You don't have to be a daredevil to have an adventurous soul. Figure out what makes you come alive. What is fun to you? What makes you smile? How can you use that to bring adventure to yourself, your family, and your community? God is unfolding your story, and if you are willing to walk forward in faith, your life *will* be an adventure.

Go deeper by meditating on Hebrews 11:8-11.

AN INVITATION TO PARIS!

Grab your kids and hunt for something French! Maybe you will discover the best croissant in your town together. Or maybe it will be the best macaron. Take a side trip to the library and check out The Little Prince *or* Madeline *or* The Story of Babar—*adventurous tales with a French twist.*

3

LEARNING TO SAVOR

JUST THINKING ABOUT the Hummingbird Room makes my mouth water.

It could have been a restaurant located anywhere in France because the menu featured French cuisine prepared by a classically trained chef who previously worked at Le Bec-Fin, a famous French restaurant in Philadelphia. Before that, Chef Eric Sarnow actually worked at two five-star restaurants in France. But the Hummingbird Room wasn't in France; it was in Spring Mills, Pennsylvania—right in my backyard.

The first time I ever went to the Hummingbird Room was when I was in high school. My boyfriend at the time took me to dinner before prom, and I had never before been to such a fancy restaurant. The setting was a beautiful old Victorian home, and the lighting was romantic and subdued. All of the waiters and waitresses wore black bow ties, white shirts, black vests, and black pants, and brought the food to the table on silver platters covered with silver domes. It was all new to me, and I loved it.

We ordered the prix-fixe meal, which included salad, bread, caviar, a salmon tart, duck, scalloped potatoes, and crème brûlée. I had never tasted anything more succulent and delicious in my entire life. The salmon tart alone was to die for, with its perfectly delicious creamy center, tender meat, and flaky-but-not-dry crust.

When the waiter served us, he pulled off the dome with a touch of the dramatic and said, "Voilà!" I fell in love. Everything was amazing. Well, *almost* everything.

I didn't want to eat the caviar.

My boyfriend said, "You have to try it."

"I am not eating caviar."

"You have to eat it."

"I'm not going to eat it."

"Put it in your mouth. We're at a nice restaurant. If you don't eat it, you will offend the chef."

"Fine!"

I put the little black fish eggs in my mouth and immediately spit them back out on my plate because I just couldn't do it! Clearly *I was so refined*. My boyfriend, who was mortified, reached over, grabbed the caviar off my plate with his hand, and put it in his mouth!

I was stunned.

He swallowed it and gave me a death stare. I think I giggled. He was not happy. Our relationship didn't last, but my love of the Hummingbird Room did. It became a favorite treat for me, and I visited it several more times. To this day I have not experienced the delight of food that I enjoyed there.

The Hummingbird Room ignited my love of French cuisine, and Julia Child deepened it.

In her memoir, *My Life in France*, she describes food in the most vivid ways. You can't read her book and not drool. Here's a taste:

I closed my eyes and inhaled the rising perfume. Then I lifted a forkful of fish to my mouth, took a bite, and chewed slowly. The flesh of the sole was delicate, with a light but distinct taste of the ocean that blended marvelously with the browned butter. I chewed slowly and swallowed. It was a morsel of perfection.[1]

There is something to closing your eyes and really savoring your food, like I instructed my kiddos to do when we went to Dosie Dough. It gives an opportunity to think about the tastes and textures and aromas. My daughter Caroline is good at savoring. At meals, she takes her time and lingers over her food when everyone else is finished. I am used to living in a culture that shovels food in without really taking the time to taste it and experience it. That's one of the things that draws me to France; the people take their time. Their meals consist of multiple courses served one at a time so you can enjoy each morsel for what it alone offers. Nothing is hurried. I want more of that slow savoring in my life, so I've decided to pay more attention to how I eat in order to bring some Paris to my everyday life.

THE GOOD STUFF

Mangez bien!

Paris is famous for its sauces, cheese, oysters, truffles, and pastries. It's also famous for its three- to sometimes eleven-course meals. Parisians even have what is known as a cheese course—how fantastic is that! I've decided I simply must make time to enjoy meals like this every now and then.

Let's talk about cheese some more. I have a love affair with Boursin, a French *fromage frais* (fresh cheese). When I was in college, a friend of mine worked in a little independent cheese shop, and she introduced me to this gift of soft delectable food. Pair it with a baguette or thin crackers—*délicieux!*

Here's the thing. If I'm going to enjoy all this pastry and cheese and sauce, I can't go overboard—I'm going to have to keep things in balance. I want to have an overall healthy diet so that I can indulge here and there without guilt. The

French are known for their fresh food, and since I'm in Amish land, we have plenty of farms with fresh produce. So, my first assignment is to start paying attention to what I eat, buy local and fresh, and get used to eating it.

MY HUNT FOR ORGANIC, LOCAL PRODUCE

To begin this process, I headed to a nutrition store a few towns over from where I live.

After picking up some Ezekiel 4:9 Bread, I asked the clerk at the checkout if she knew of any organic farms in the area. Even though I live in one of the farm meccas of the world, the majority of these farmers spray some form of pesticides on their crops. However, the nice clerk told me about a little place a bit out of the way in the town of Bird-in-Hand, Pennsylvania, where they sell local organic produce. Score!

I got back in my trusty minivan, typed the address in my GPS, and started toward the cornfields.

There were fields everywhere I looked, countless acres of corn and tobacco and flowers. In between the fields, horses and cows grazed, and every so often I'd see signs for goat milk and zucchini bread. Produce stands abounded, as well as barefooted Amish children walking along the streets or in the fields. I never get tired of seeing the little boys in their straw hats, white or blue shirts, and black pants with suspenders, or the little girls with their bonnets and two long braids swinging in perpetual motion as they skip along in their homemade dresses.

It's really beautiful out here, I thought.

I kept my windows rolled down. The August air was humid, sweat beads were forming at my hairline, and I was sure my deodorant was working overtime, but I had read recently that sweating detoxifies the body, so I was intentionally baking.

I looked down and saw that my van was running on empty. (I always seemed to find myself in this predicament.) The needle on the gauge was way below E, and I was out in the cornfields.

This is not good. Should I keep going, hoping I'll run into a gas station, or turn around and go back to where I know there is one, even though I will run the risk of stalling?

I decided to go back.

I started talking to my van: "You can do it, baby. You can make it. Come on. If you make it, I will give you a name. I will name you Distance. Please, please let's not get stuck out here in the cornfields."

My van's name is now Distance because she made it to the gas station.

Whew.

In heading back toward the country, I nearly missed the turnoff. But then I spotted the sign at an intersection: Miller's Natural Foods.

Almost there.

I was now on a dirt road, with fields on my left and small

farmhouses with bikes parked outside on my right. There were miniature cornfields—garden-sized—in front of the houses. I heard a rooster crow and a baby crying. The road seemed to go on forever, but Distance and I actually traveled only about a quarter mile.

As I pulled up closer to Miller's, I saw an old Amish couple working across from the modest store. The man, who was busy hoeing in a garden, had a long white beard and was wearing a wide-brimmed straw hat, a white shirt, and black pants with suspenders. His wife was washing windows on the house. She was barefoot and dressed in a long, dark-blue dress with a black apron and a white head covering that looked like boned fishnet with long strings down the sides.

I parked Distance in the paved lot. As I walked up the steps, I noticed a sign on the door: No electric lights. *Uh-oh, no electricity? I need some relief from the heat.* Surprise—it was air-conditioned! *Huh. No electric lights, but air-conditioning.* Maybe they had some secret and it wasn't really air-conditioning. Either way, it was cool, and I was relieved. And there were enough skylights and windows providing natural light inside so I wasn't wandering around in the dark.

The first thing I noticed was homemade bread. Homemade bread made by the Amish! That sounded appealing, so I picked up a loaf, scanned the ingredient list, and was tickled that I knew what each ingredient was. I had found my natural food mecca. I decided to buy a couple of loaves, placing them in my wire shopping basket, and then headed for the produce section of the store.

I walked through long plastic strips into a room-sized cooler—it was freezing in there. The strawberries and blueberries immediately caught my eye.

Hmmm, the prices aren't bad at all.

I grabbed a few containers of berries. All around me were shelves loaded with bulk items in clear bags: oats, flour, dried fruit, nuts, and seeds. There was so much variety that three of the four walls were stacked with these bags. On the other wall was a refrigerated case with organic milk, almond milk, cheeses, butter, and all sorts of organic fare. I added green peppers and spinach to my basket, and as I walked around to where the bananas were, I passed a shelf that nearly intoxicated me with glorious smells of chocolate and coconut and dried fruit. I paused and just took it in for a moment.

Where is that wonderful aroma coming from? I don't see any chocolate. Where are they hiding the chocolate?

I retraced my steps back through the hanging plastic strips, and my goose bumps disappeared. Back in the front of the store, there were shelves of cereal, granola, snacks, maple syrup, honey, chips, macaroni and cheese, spaghetti sauce, and all sorts of natural, organic items. There were essential oils, vitamins, deodorant, and bars of soap.

On the way to the checkout, I snatched a bar of 85 percent dark chocolate. *Yum.*

An Amish girl stood behind the counter. Her hair was pulled tightly back behind her white head covering. She had no makeup on. She was wearing a long buttoned-down light purple dress that reached to her ankles, with a black apron tied around her waist. She also had on low-cut black socks and black sneakers.

I put my healthy bounty on the counter, and she rang me up.

"That will be forty-one dollars."

Okay, I can deal with that.

I opened my wallet and handed her my debit card.

She stared at me.

"We only take cash or check."

Her Dutch accent was thick but quite lovely.

"Do you have an ATM?"

More staring.

Clearly, something was wrong with me.

I smiled at her. "Can you tell me where I might find one nearby?"

She proceeded to give me directions using *cornfields* as landmarks. I kid you not. It was something like this (in that wonderful Dutch accent):

"Take the road down to the cornfield on the left, and then take a right at the cornfield on the corner, and then you'll be on a road by a cornfield. Keep going, and take a left by the big cornfield, another right, and then a left, and then it will be past the cornfield on your way to town."

Right.

I got in my car and thanked God for GPS because . . . *cornfields.*

I would like to state again that something was obviously wrong with *me*, not her. I mean, who goes to an Amish store in the middle of cornfields and asks about an ATM?

It's amazing I function in life.

I headed back to the town beyond the cornfields and found a grocery store with an ATM, got cash, and went back to Miller's to pay for my Amish goods.

And now I have a local place to buy organic in the future.

I'll just make sure to bring cash next time.

THE TEN DAYS I THOUGHT WOULD NEVER END
(aka The Most Boring Diet Ever)

Now that I had my fresh produce and was paying attention to living healthily in order to indulge, I decided to enter Phase 2 of my experiment: eating a plant-based diet for ten days. And by plant-based, I mean a version of the Daniel Diet, which is basically vegan with no fun. More specifically, it's a whole-grains, vegetables, and fruits diet. No sweets allowed, not even honey. This diet would serve as a detox of sorts, preparing my body for massive French cheese intake.

The Daniel Diet is based on Daniel 1:8-16 and Daniel 10:3. For ten days Daniel and his friends, captives of King Nebuchadnezzar in Babylon, refused to eat the king's food. They didn't eat any meat—just vegetables and water—in obedience to God. At the end of the ten days, they looked healthier than the men who ate meat and all the king's food:

At the end of ten days their appearance seemed better and they were fatter than all the youths who had been eating the king's choice food.

DANIEL 1:15

There is obviously much more to this story (I encourage you to read all about Daniel's amazing life), but for me it was just a starting point. I wanted to see if I could undertake such a challenge and if I would feel healthier and more energized at the end. Again, in order to reward myself with cheese.

The first five days were hard because, well, *bacon*. I missed the bacon. And the toast and the eggs and pretty much everything else. On the upside, I lost four pounds. I also felt fantastic, energized, and full. I was surprised by the full thing; I thought for sure I'd feel hungry on this diet.

The next five days were much easier, and in fact, I began to actually like eating my daily Ezekiel 4:9 cereal (sans milk) with a banana for breakfast, stir-fry for lunch, and a dinner that seemed to always involve some type of beans, whole-grain rice, and spinach or other nutritious vegetables.

By the end of the ten days, I felt awesome. And the best part? I lost all my cravings. It was so strange to not crave anything.

In fact, I liked how I felt so much, that I planned on continuing to eat a mainly plant-based diet for the rest of my life.

But then I had bacon—and cheese—and it was all over.

Here's my conclusion: Plants are great, but so is cheese. I'll take it all.

But to take it all, I needed to think about exercising. Which really was the problem—I *think* about it and don't actually *do* it. Le sigh. My next experiment was clear . . .

GET A MOVE ON!

I'm a wimp.

I really don't like exercising because I don't like pain. As I mentioned earlier, I'd rather sit unbothered in my comfy chair with coffee and a book . . . and cheese.

Running?

Boring.

Swimming?

Cold and wet.

Dancing?

Requires coordination.

I had to try something. *Walking on a treadmill might be tolerable if I have an audio book to listen to while I'm treading. Maybe I could do that.*

But first, I agreed to check out the Body Pump class at a local gym, recommended by a friend. Her description made it sound fun.

That week I joined the gym and went to Body Pump. Afterward I was sore, but it was . . . okay. The highlight for me was seeing an old man wearing a sweatband in the class.

I think I might wear a sweatband the next time I go.

My enthusiasm for exercise slowly began to grow. One morning, I had a novel idea.

I'm going to take a walk today.

After fifteen minutes, I actually had an urge to jog, so I did. I even broke out in a tiny sweat. Jesse was impressed, although he teased me the rest of the afternoon, making comments such as, "Have you ever sweated before?"

⁓

My gym membership was short-lived. It was affecting the family budget, and I just couldn't squeeze it in. Good-bye, treadmill. Good-bye, Body Pump. Good-bye, man with the sweatband.

I wasn't ready to throw in the towel yet. I am an Amazon Prime member, which means I receive free shipping on things I order *and* have access to free movies, including workout videos. Dilemma solved! *Now, who do I want to sweat with?*

I typed in "exercise workouts" and up popped Jillian Michaels. I read the descriptions of the free ones that looked interesting, but all of them were more than fifty minutes long. *No can do as a mother of three young kiddos.* Besides, Jillian's so intense! I wasn't ready for her.

I needed something with a title like *30-Minute Workout for the Aged.*

I kept scrolling through the freebies until I landed on the only option that fit my criteria: *Billy Blanks Jr.: Dance Party Boot Camp.*

Wait, Billy Blanks has a son who teaches fitness?

I remembered when Billy Blanks Sr. taught Tae Bo, and it was *all the craze.* Now I really felt old.

But Billy Blanks Jr. would have to instruct me this time.

Being terribly uncoordinated, I knew this was going to be very interesting.

The next morning I got up at 5:30 a.m., made a cup of coffee, and read my Bible in bed while sipping on my coffee. Then I read a few chapters of a book on habits. At around 7 a.m. I told my kiddos I was going to work out and they were welcome to join in or watch.

"I promise it will be hilarious."

I made it through only twenty minutes of Billy Blanks Jr.'s thirty-nine-minute cardio workout. My oldest daughter secretly filmed me. I was humiliated. I realized I'd have to get good at the moves from the first half before I could finish the whole thirty-nine minutes.

Day 2, I gave up on Billy. *Sorry, Billy, I wasn't into it at all.* Instead, I watched a documentary (something about the history of our country) while jogging in place, doing a set of jumping jacks, and moving different parts of my body for about a half hour. Once again, I looked ridiculous on the secret video footage my daughter took and showed me later.

Day 3 was Day 2 all over again.

Day 4 never happened.

Then I bought a stair stepper. I kid you not. The small kind that barely moves. My dear friend Ginny laughed when she saw it and said, "You do realize that's not an exercise machine—that's a joke!"

Ha.

It's now sitting in my closet collecting dust. Sigh.

Was I doomed to never exercise consistently? I needed to know what French women do.

FRENCH WOMEN, EXERCISE, AND PLEASURE

Okay, French women, with your sleek curves, late-night eating, and cheese. How do you do it?

According to Mireille Guiliano, author of *French Women Don't Get Fat*,

> Even in exercise, start with pleasure. . . . American women seem to have two modes: sitting or spinning. French women prefer the gentler, more regular varieties of all-day movement—"the slow burn" in American terms. And as you might expect, our approach, true to Cartesian principles, demands that you use your mind as you use your body. Mindless exercise is almost as bad as mindless eating. We strive to diversify the physical movement in our lives and practice it as second nature. And we cultivate awareness as we go.[2]

I think this philosophy makes a ton of sense. I like the idea of a well-rounded attitude toward having a healthy body, particularly because we've already established my dislike of pain in working out. But walking, cleaning, living . . . just having a life where I move throughout the day is good and fitting.

I've decided to be more French when it comes to a healthy

body. No more Billy Blanks Jr., no more sweatbands, no more stair stepper. Yes to the "slow burn."

INDULGING

Since I'm on the lookout for ways to be intentional with eating and savoring, I was thrilled to be invited to a friend's house for a five-course meal. Let me tell you all about it . . .

It was a beautiful fall evening, with just enough chill in the air to have the fire pit lit up. When Jesse and I arrived, we were directed to a table set up on the deck with homemade guacamole, salsa, and Welsh rarebit with toasted baguette slices and wine. Our host said, "Just enjoy the company before we begin." There were ten of us standing around sampling the appetizers, not including all the children who happily ran around playing with each other.

About forty-five minutes later, we headed inside to sit down for the first course: salad. We crowded around the table and enjoyed the sweet and salty tastes of greens tossed with figs, feta cheese, bacon, cherry juice–infused Craisins, and a homemade balsamic vinaigrette. We delighted in rosemary bread fresh from the oven, dipping it in olive oil mixed with spices. We talked and laughed and took our time. After a while we had soup—a delicious smoked chicken corn chowder. The main course was grilled top sirloin steak, given an Argentinean twist with homemade chimichurri sauce and served with a side of rice topped with fresh pico de gallo and grilled sweet peppers. (Are you hungry yet?) There was more talking and laughing before the dessert finale of warm apple crisp with fresh whipped cream, and a pumpkin cake with cream-cheese icing—all homemade of course.

We had arrived at 5:30 and didn't leave until nearly midnight. It was an evening of utter satisfaction.

ᥱᦵᦵ

In keeping with this willingness to find satisfaction by taking my time to savor food, I decided to continue the experiment at the Lititz Family Cupboard restaurant, where my husband and I were starting a daylong anniversary celebration with breakfast out. The Family Cupboard is known for its all-you-care-to-eat buffet, and that is exactly what Jesse decided to get. I chose the quiche.

I took a bite of my quiche and ate it slowly, relishing in each cheesy bit. Jesse sat across from me, his plate filled with eggs and bacon and toast and pancakes and all sorts of food from the delicious selection.

When Jesse started talking, I quickly interrupted.

"Honey, could you please be quiet, just for a moment, so I can really taste my food?"

I needed silence.

There is something about eating without talking that helps me fully engage with my food. This sounds weird, I know, but I don't care. My quiche was wonderful and I wanted to enjoy it fully, because secretly I was pretending I was in a Parisian café, and I was eating a French quiche made fresh that morning.

My eyes were closed. I heard a chair move, and I opened my eyes.

Jesse was heading back to the *buffet* (that's an eighteenth-century French word, by the way)—I had stopped counting how many times he'd filled his plate.

Finally I said to my loving husband, "Listen, you have to tell me when you're making your last stop at the buffet because that's when I'm going to eat the crust."

I had just brought a touch of Paris to a little breakfast in this Lancaster County restaurant. It was so good. And I realized then that it didn't matter if I was in a café in Paris or in Pennsylvania Dutch country thousands of miles away. The quiche was just as enjoyable because of the way I savored it. I chose to eat it as though I was served in a French café. And it was perfect.

Plus, my gracious and handsome company made it all the more *magnifique*.

After having such lovely food experiences, I have decided to begin cooking something new at least once a month. I am also going to let go of my hesitations of inviting people over to our small home and, instead, create an atmosphere of hospitality and good food. If I don't get over my fears and get on with enjoying life with friends and culinary delights, I'm just going to waste many good years waiting for the right house or the right time or enough money. It may never happen, so I'm going to choose to live now with what I have and where I am.

Here's to savoring life!

༉ *Unearthing Your Longings*

Just think, God could have made food boring, colorless, and tasteless. But instead He created taste buds so we could relish thousands of flavors in foods of all colors and textures, foods that not only help our bodies thrive but that we can enjoy and take pleasure in. When you enjoy food, you are enjoying the kindness of the Lord. Look around you. What other kindnesses of the Lord can you see? He gave them to you because *He loves you.*

Go deeper by meditating on Psalm 34:8, Psalm 63:5, and Psalm 119:103.

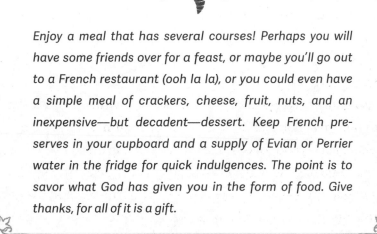

AN INVITATION TO PARIS!

Enjoy a meal that has several courses! Perhaps you will have some friends over for a feast, or maybe you'll go out to a French restaurant (ooh la la), or you could even have a simple meal of crackers, cheese, fruit, nuts, and an inexpensive—but decadent—dessert. Keep French preserves in your cupboard and a supply of Evian or Perrier water in the fridge for quick indulgences. The point is to savor what God has given you in the form of food. Give thanks, for all of it is a gift.

⟪ 4 ⟫

BEAUTY

I'VE NEVER MET a French woman in person.

My knowledge of French women comes from books, movies, the Internet, and bits of information gleaned from my mom's impressions as a girl living in France for two years. But even without these resources, I've always sensed that a French woman's beauty radiates from a confidence in who she is. It isn't so much about how she looks as it is in how she carries herself—with a strong sense of knowing herself, accepting herself, and growing more into who she is.

In Debra Ollivier's book, *Entre Nous: A Woman's Guide to Finding Her Inner French Girl*, she describes the quintessential French woman:

She is entirely, unequivocally self-contained. She is focused on living her own full life, following her own agenda and cultivating her actual self, rather than reinventing herself or pining away to be someone she's not. Throughout her life, she invests herself in learning and experiencing, not to *change* who she is, but to *become* more fundamentally and more fully who she truly is. . . . She is imbued with a strength of character and a certain sensitivity. Because she is sure of who she is on the inside, she naturally, inevitably, appears sure of herself on the outside.[3]

If you read this quickly, you might think a French woman is just selfish and humanistic. But the overall sense that I get is that she exemplifies *freedom*—in who she is and in who she would like to be.

As a Christian who has been redeemed in Christ, who has been made in the image of God, with gifts of purpose and a personality that has been woven together by God Himself, I should be able to be free to live out of who God made me to be. Instead of trying to change or be like someone else, I want to mature—with the help of the Holy Spirit—in holiness. I want to be who God made me to be: colorful and beautiful and gifted, which brings me pleasure and Him glory.

As I ponder beauty and confidence and personality and glory and holiness, I'm wondering how I can bring these things to a daily realization in my life. I want to carry myself with confidence in who I am; I want to embrace beauty because God made it. I don't want to base my identity on physical beauty, because it's vain and fleeting, but I want to enjoy beauty because it is pleasing to God to have me take pleasure in it. With all of these swirling thoughts in my mind, I have decided that I want to pursue a deeper beauty, one that comes from communing with the beautiful One. Therefore I will seek His face intentionally, to cherish the true beauty He tucked inside me in order to appreciate it more fully.

> *My heart says of you, "Seek his face!"*
> *Your face, LORD, I will seek.*
> PSALM 27:8, NIV

My friend Soleil told me that God is like the ocean.

We may be standing in the water up to our necks, pushed off our feet by each wave, tasting the salt, stretching our fingertips through the undulating water as far as they can go, but even after all of that, we have not yet fully experienced the ocean.

We have not experienced an ocean's expansiveness or depth—its fathoms and fullness—and if we were to continue exploring, our experience would be different than the time before. If we dived five feet down, the deep water and the marine life that occupies it would be new, and if we donned scuba gear and plunged a hundred feet further, everything would be new again.

It is so vast and mysterious and untamable and surprising.
I have no idea who my God really is.
But He is like the ocean.
And my mind cannot contain the fullness of Him.

> *Great is our Lord and mighty in power;*
> *his understanding has no limit.*

PSALM 147:5, NIV

For me, seeking God's face is going farther into the ocean.
It's searching, yearning for more intimacy.

> *Then you will call upon me and come and pray to*
> *me, and I will hear you. You will seek me and find*
> *me, when you seek me with all your heart. I will be*
> *found by you, declares the LORD, and I will restore your*
> *fortunes and gather you from all the nations and all the*
> *places where I have driven you, declares the LORD, and*
> *I will bring you back to the place from which I sent you*
> *into exile.*

JEREMIAH 29:12-14, ESV

Seeking God's face is about entering into God's presence.

Seeking the *Lord* means seeking his *presence.*
"Presence" is a common translation of the Hebrew
word "face." Literally, we are to seek his "face." But
this is the Hebraic way of having access to God.

To be before his *face* is to be in his presence. . . . God's manifest, conscious, trusted presence is not our constant experience. There are seasons when we become neglectful of God and give him no thought and do not put trust in him and we find him "unmanifested"—that is, unperceived as great and beautiful and valuable by the eyes of our hearts.

His face—the brightness of his personal character—is hidden behind the curtain of our carnal desires. This condition is always ready to overtake us. That is why we are told to "seek his presence *continually*." God calls us to enjoy continual consciousness of his supreme greatness and beauty and worth.[4]

This is my heart's desire . . .

> *Now set your mind and heart to seek the LORD your God.*
> I CHRONICLES 22:19, ESV

> *If you seek him, he will be found by you.*
> I CHRONICLES 28:9, ESV

> *Seek the LORD while he may be found; call upon him while he is near.*
> ISAIAH 55:6, ESV

Moses spent forty days on a mountain with God, and when he came down, his face literally shone; he actually had to put on a veil because he had been with the living God face-to-face, and the glow that remained from that encounter scared people.

Then the LORD said to Moses, "Write down these
words, for in accordance with these words I have
made a covenant with you and with Israel." So
he was there with the LORD forty days and forty
nights; he did not eat bread or drink water. And he
wrote on the tablets the words of the covenant, the
Ten Commandments.

It came about when Moses was coming down
from Mount Sinai (and the two tablets of the
testimony were in Moses' hand as he was coming down
from the mountain), that Moses did not know that the
skin of his face shone because of his speaking with Him.
So when Aaron and all the sons of Israel saw Moses,
behold, the skin of his face shone, and they were afraid
to come near him. Then Moses called to them, and
Aaron and all the rulers in the congregation returned
to him; and Moses spoke to them. Afterward all the
sons of Israel came near, and he commanded them to
do everything that the LORD had spoken to him on
Mount Sinai. When Moses had finished speaking with
them, he put a veil over his face. But whenever Moses
went in before the LORD to speak with Him, he would

take off the veil until he came out; and whenever he came out and spoke to the sons of Israel what he had been commanded, the sons of Israel would see the face of Moses, that the skin of Moses' face shone. So Moses would replace the veil over his face until he went in to speak with Him.

EXODUS 34:27-35

I love that Scripture because, first of all, Moses was with God for forty days. When Moses came down from the mountain, there was no question that he had been with God—*the* Light. It was "written" all over his face! Moses' countenance reflected the light, and his face literally shone. It radiated so much that the dramatic change scared the people of Israel, and their leader had to wear a veil while he talked to them. Whenever Moses returned to the mountain to speak with the Lord, he would remove the veil while he was in God's presence and put it back on when he stood before the Israelites.

That same divine radiance was on Stephen's face when he was arrested on false charges and brought before the high council to be judged:

And gazing at him, all who sat in the council saw that his face was like the face of an angel. . . . Now when they heard these things they were enraged, and they ground their teeth at him. But he, full of the Holy Spirit, gazed into heaven and saw the glory of God, and

> *Jesus standing at the right hand of God. And he said,*
> *"Behold, I see the heavens opened, and the Son of Man*
> *standing at the right hand of God."*
> ACTS 6:15; 7:54-56, ESV

I am convinced that Stephen's face shone like that of Moses.

So here's the thing: Moses and Stephen each spent time alone with God, and because of that time, people who saw each of them knew that this person had encountered the living God. And if we take the time to seek God's face, to search for that communion and intimacy, I wonder if we will also shine so that when people see us they will know that we have encountered the living God.

When we look for Him, pushing all hindrances aside; when we aim for and keep our eyes on Jesus, letting nothing compare to Him, then I think we will be fully made available to Him, for Him. And we will change the world because God needs available people to be devoted and dedicated, laid open and vulnerable before Him so that in our weakness He is made strong. His power will come through us, and we will be able to do *real* Kingdom work, the kind that urges us out of our comfort zones and ourselves. We will be available to be completely used by Him. As one of my favorite authors, A. W. Tozer says,

> Let the old saints be our example. They came to the
> Word of God and meditated. They laid their Bible

on the old-fashioned handmade chair, got down on the old scrubbed wooden floor and meditated on the Word. As they waited, faith mounted. The Spirit and faith illuminated. Their only Bible had fine print, narrow margins, and poor paper, but they knew their Bible better than some of us do, even with all of our modern "helps."

Let's practice the art of Bible meditation. . . . Let us open our Bibles, spread them out on a chair, and meditate on the Word of God. It will open itself to us, and the Spirit of God will come and brood over it.[5]

GETTING QUIET WITH GOD

My desire for closeness with God led me to twenty days of purposeful, quiet time seeking His face.

I decided one of the ways to seek His face was to meditate, which simply means to revolve something in the mind; to contemplate.

I wanted to ponder God and His world and His Word.

In his book *Celebration of Discipline*, Richard Foster says that Christians through the ages have made it a practice to meditate. And it is as simple as this:

Christian meditation . . . is the ability to hear God's voice and obey his word.[6]

I wanted to feast on God's Word, hear Him, sense Him, and heed the life He calls me to.

Entering into the sacred quiet was my gateway to remembering who He is. There I pondered His truths and opened myself up to listening, making room for communion with the divine.

Before you wonder if I went off the deep end, hear me out, please. I am not talking about anything other than engaging in a form of quiet, still prayer. As I contemplated God and His Word, I inevitably began to talk with Him.

I'll be honest with you: In the past I rarely made time for meditation. I was too busy, too bothered, too *distracted*. Everything else seemed more interesting . . . more entertaining.

Sitting and contemplating is a discipline because it does not come easy; God is not with us to entertain us.

I quickly found myself wondering, *What can I do to become more disciplined, to conquer my lack of focus? How can I meditate in an age of massive distraction?*

DEATHBLOW TO DISTRACTIONS

Prone to wander, Lord, I feel it.
Prone to leave the God I love;
Here's my heart, O take and seal it.
Seal it for Thy courts above.[7]

Oh yes, distractions. I easily become fickle in my devotion to God, quickly swayed by whatever is shiny and interesting to me, lulling me away from my God. Tozer reminds me that my distractions are not a thing to take lightly.

Among the enemies to devotion none is so harmful as distractions. Whatever excites the curiosity, scatters the thoughts, disquiets the heart, absorbs the interests or shifts our life focus from the kingdom of God within us to the world around us—that is a distraction; and the world is full of them. Our science-based civilization has given us many benefits but it has multiplied our distractions and so taken away far more than it has given. . . .

The remedy for distractions is the same now as it was in earlier and simpler times, viz., prayer, meditation and the cultivation of the inner life. The psalmist said "Be still, and know," and Christ told us to enter into our closet, shut the door and pray unto the Father. It still works. . . .

Distractions *must* be conquered or they will conquer us. So let us cultivate simplicity; let us want fewer things; let us walk in the Spirit; let us fill our minds with the Word of God and our hearts with praise. In that way we can live in peace even in such a distraught world as this.[8]

My biggest distraction by far is the Internet. There are blogs and news pieces and Facebook and

Twitter and opinions and debates and . . . well, Viral-Nova and Buzzfeed.

Entertainment. It's easy, and it doesn't require anything from me . . . except my time. Which, of course, becomes my life.

But, of course, the real problem isn't the entertainment; it is my lust for it and my lack of self-discipline.

And I don't just lack self-discipline when it comes to being entertained; I lack it in good things as well. Reading, for example.

Reading is a great hobby, but if you spend all your time reading books and avoiding God, it is an unhealthy distraction.

Actually, doing too much of anything at the expense of getting quiet with the One who knows the depths of your soul is to forfeit the gospel. It is to forfeit the beauty we have before us and in us and that, when cultivated through the work of the Holy Spirit, will shine out of us.

The power of the gospel draws us into a living relationship with our Maker, leading us to reach out to others, to serve and share our hope, and to meet the needs of the needy. The light of Jesus Christ in us will certainly be hidden under the proverbial bushel if we become sidetracked.

> Anything that keeps me from knowing God is my enemy, and any gift that comes between Him and me is my enemy.[9]

What does that look like?

It means giving my soul what it needs, which is time and

space with the One who fashioned it. It also means stepping away from the Internet and choosing to get quiet and still.

❧

During my twenty days of seeking God's face, one of the things I did was take one week and meditate each day.

Here is what that looked like:

I got quiet in my comfy brown couch with my legs up on the recliner, head back, and eyes closed. I thought about Psalm 1:2-3:

> *His delight is in the law of the* LORD,
> *and in His law he meditates day and night.*
> *He will be like a tree firmly planted by streams*
> *   of water,*
> *which yields its fruit in its season*
> *and its leaf does not wither;*
> *and in whatever he does, he prospers.*

Richard Foster says it's okay to use your God-given imagination when you meditate. I decided to try it. I pictured myself in a beautiful place—a Monet-like meadow—with green fields and flowers and a weeping willow. I was going to meet Jesus there.

But I struggled to stay focused.

So I decided to pray instead. "God, I just want to know You're with me."

I know it's silly for a Christian to say that, because God is always with me; He never leaves me. But I guess what I was really saying was that I wanted to *feel* Him with me. I wanted to sit in His presence and know it.

Thoughts crowded my mind. *Maybe God doesn't speak anymore. Or maybe He only speaks to really special chosen people. And how does He "speak" to people anyway?* I wasn't expecting to hear an audible voice, but I was certain He would speak to my spirit. I have experienced that at different times in my life, and I longed for it again.

"God, I'd like to know I'm not alone here."

It was around this point when my son woke up, found where I was, and cuddled up next to me. I ended my meditation session and opened up my daily e-mail devotional.

The Scripture in it? Psalm 27:8.

> My heart says of you, "Seek his face!"
>   Your face, LORD, I will seek. (NIV)

I was stunned. *Yes, yes, that's what I am trying to do.* I eagerly read on, resonating with a quote from Tozer:

> The great of the kingdom have been those who loved God more than others did. . . . The one vital quality which they had in common was spiritual receptivity. Something in them was open to heaven, something which urged them Godward.[10]

I am urged Godward . . . and the Lord knows I'm open to heaven. But do I love Him the most? Have I sought after His face?

I know God used those words to speak directly to me. I know it. And I cried, because I knew He had heard me, and He had answered my cry.

"What's wrong, Mommy? Why are you crying?" Caed asked me, his small voice starting to choke up.

I hugged him, putting his concern to rest. "Mommy's okay, honey. These are happy tears because God spoke to me."

Caed smiled and nodded.

It happened again the next day . . . the Lord gently wooing me.

A babysitter was watching the kiddos so I could have writing time for this book, and while they were outside, I decided to seize the opportunity and spend a few minutes meditating. My devotional that morning had come from Genesis 35.

Jacob had been given specific instructions by God to pack up and move, and then he explained to his entire household what was happening.

We are now going to Bethel, where I will build an altar to the God who answered my prayers when I was in distress. He has been with me wherever I have gone.

GENESIS 35:3, NLT

The stone pillar Jacob eventually sets up is a reminder of God's fulfilled promise to him. The devotional writer pointed out that all of us should have things to remind us of what God has done in our lives. I paged back to the end of Genesis 32 for context, the account of Jacob wrestling with God. And there it was—Jacob's bold statement:

> *I have seen God face to face.*
> GENESIS 32:30

I stopped, overwhelmed. In that moment I can only say I felt as if I were being filled with the Holy Spirit, being stirred in my soul. I practically shook. I had to go down to my bedroom and lock the door so I could cry. I felt so overcome by the Lord, and I knew He was speaking to me, letting me know that He hears me. Two days in a row, He answered the cry of my heart to see Him. I didn't need to see Him physically because to seek His face is to be so close, to be intimate, to know Him who is in me. And it had happened. He met me when I sought after Him, thirsty to know Him more. Oh friends, our God is good and kind, and He wants us to seek Him. As the psalmist says,

> *As the deer longs for streams of water,*
> *so I long for you, O God.*
> *I thirst for God, the living God.*
> PSALM 42:1-2, NLT

What are you thirsty for?

I discovered a prayer room in my area. Well, *discovered* isn't completely accurate.

I have a friend who told me about a dance class for my daughter that was held at a place called Gateway, and I began taking her there once a week. I knew there was a prayer room in the same building, but I never thought much about it—until I received some bad news on a day when my daughter had dance class. That day happened to be during my twenty days of seeking God's face.

I was a wreck emotionally. I didn't know what to do except to go to the prayer room. I just sat and listened as a young man sang, and I cried and prayed and allowed God's peace to settle over me in that place. It was exactly what I needed.

The prayer room is open 24/7. Sometimes they have live worship, sometimes they have recorded music, sometimes many people are there, and sometimes it's nearly empty. But it's a quiet space; there is a peace about it. Children are welcome there. They have a special table set up for anyone who wants to draw or paint, and my children love that area. Sometimes my kiddos sit and listen to someone sing, sometimes they dance, sometimes they create. One time my son even took the microphone and started praying.

I have found a spiritual home in the prayer room and, Lord willing, I believe it will be a refuge for years to come.

AN AWAKENED HEART IS A BEAUTIFUL THING
(Looking for the Beauty of the Lord)

As I mentioned earlier, the summer between my junior and senior years of college I went to Memphis, Tennessee, to work at a kid's camp.

On weekends and on some evenings I would have free time to go, get lost, and explore the city. During one of my explorations, I came across a coffee shop called Java Cabana— a little place filled with character and warmth. There were a few small tables and chairs and comfy armchairs and couches. Art pieces from local artisans decorated the walls, and used books filled the shelves. I wasn't drinking coffee at the time (I didn't start drinking coffee until I had my second child), so I ordered the Lisa-Marie, which was a chai hot chocolate with sprinkles and loads of whipped cream.

On that initial visit, I found a spot on one of the couches, made myself comfortable, and picked up a journal from the nearby coffee table. Some pages were written on, while others had drawings. *This is a communal journal*, I thought, *shared by anyone and everyone who comes into the coffee shop.* As I slowly turned the pages, I became lost in the thoughts of strangers. Poetry, art, stories, quotes, and ramblings filled the pages; I was fascinated. I picked up another journal that had blank pages, and I wrote something too. I don't remember what I wrote, but I know that I gave a piece of myself to others that day.

I went back to that coffee shop several times over the

summer, and one evening I witnessed my first open mic night. People were getting up and reading poetry; I had never seen this before. One man in particular named Christian got my attention. He wore baggy clothing and had spiky blond hair. He stood in front of the mic, and out of his mouth came an art form I had never heard before: slam poetry.

I was taken aback and awestruck simultaneously. His words, the passion behind them, the heartache—I could feel it all. He was vulnerable and honest and sharp. I loved it. Afterward I went up to him.

"Thank you so much for sharing your poems, Christian. I have never heard anything like them before. Do you have a collection of your poetry in a book? I would love to buy it if you do." He said he was going to self-publish, and when he completed it, he would send me a copy, which he did.

Christian was kind and open. He had struggled with drugs and had been in and out of jail. I had never met anyone like him, someone who was willing to share his deepest demons.

Java Cabana and the culture I experienced there was something that dug into my soul and opened it up. My summer in Memphis was the catalyst that awakened my spirit to art and culture and poetry that was beautifully transparent in its brokenness. Looking back, I think that's the reason God arranged for me to be there—not for the camp, although that was good, but for the awakening.

That summer, art healed a part of me and made me courageous enough to share some of my own story with others.

It helped me to be okay when I wasn't. It helped me to love the broken and to see humanness mixed with glory.

Through the awakening of my heart, I found I was able to relate to and comfort others.

c2⁹

After graduating from college, I got a job as a counselor at a crisis pregnancy clinic. One day a mom came in with her sixteen-year-old daughter. Her daughter wasn't pregnant, but her mom was concerned for her. She felt like her daughter was emotionally closed off and spending time with the wrong types of people.

"I'm at the end of my rope," the mother said. "I didn't know where else to turn. Do you think you could talk to her about what could happen if she keeps going down this path?"

"I will certainly try."

When Lucy (not her real name) came into the room, it was awkward. She clearly did not want to be there. I decided to break the silence by telling her a little bit about myself.

Then I said, "What's your favorite ice cream?"

There was a hint of a smile. "Raspberry."

For whatever reason I thought to myself, *I bet a girl who likes raspberry ice cream likes poetry too.*

We talked for a few minutes more and scheduled a time to get together again.

The next time Lucy and I met, we sat outside the office at a picnic table. I surprised her with some raspberry ice cream. She smiled because I remembered. As we were enjoying our tartly sweet treat, I pulled out a journal of my poetry. Ever since being introduced to slam poetry at Java Cabana in Memphis, I had begun writing my own. I had never shown it or shared it with anyone else, but this seemed like the right place and the right person to do just that.

I began to read the poems that had come from deep places in my heart, becoming more vulnerable with each line.

It took only a few minutes for Lucy's walls to crumble. She shared with me her writings and poetry, and we talked about all sorts of things. I listened to her, and she began to trust me.

I spoke life into her when she allowed me to, or when she asked me questions, but mostly I just wanted to love her for who she was and where she was. We met several times after this, in the office, at the park, and we just talked about life. I think she just needed someone to listen to her and accept her for who she was. Eventually our time together ended. I never saw her again, but I know I was able to be a friend to her when she needed one.

Before our last meeting, she gave me a copy of her favorite book. It was her way of saying "Thank you" and "Now you understand a piece of me."

I don't know where she is today, but she stays with me, and my hope is that something I offered has stayed with her.

What I saw in Lucy was the beauty of the Lord, hidden behind a sixteen-year-old with long hair and a quiet spirit. She was bursting with hidden beauty, and it's that beauty

I want to always see in people; it's what I want my children to be able to see. Behind the masks and the pain and whatever else is on the outside, I want us to see the imprint of God on everyone.

And I want to see it in all of the world. There is so much bad, but there is so much glory as well.

> Beautiful faces are they that wear
>> The light of a pleasant spirit there;
> Beautiful hands are they that do
>> Deeds that are noble, kind and true;
> Beautiful feet are they that go
>> Swiftly to lighten another's woe.
>
> MCGUFFEY'S SECOND READER[11]

God placed so much color in this world—beautiful, breathtaking, wild, fun, intriguing, surprising color. Color in the sky and in skin and in personalities. I'm looking for it and listening for it and trying to awaken it within my children too.

I asked my children to listen to a piece of music with their eyes closed. "Do you hear the different instruments? What sounds do you hear? How does it make you feel?"

Another day I made them close their eyes as I read a poem to them. "What do you see? What do you hear in the words?"

In these still moments, they can see the beauty.

The challenge is teaching my children how to be still. I'm working on it.

I want my children to know how to lie down in a field without feeling fidgety, to relax under the expanse of the wild blue as they feel the wind tickle their noses. Giggles are permitted and encouraged.

And art. I want them to see God's beauty in art.

⁊

My favorite artist is Claude Monet. When I go to Paris one day, I will take a little side trip to Giverny where he lived and painted. He planned his gardens for the purposes of symmetry and color, creating his own landscapes to paint. One thing that I particularly love about him is that he painted normal everyday things. He brought them to life and made them really beautiful. He painted what he saw out his backdoor, and he captured his children and wife in natural settings, doing things that a mother and her children would normally do.

One particular painting he did of his wife—*Camille on Her Deathbed*—brings tears to my eyes. You can see how heartbroken Monet was when he captured that moment, but even so, it's beautiful.

While I love Monet, I am also drawn to the works of Rembrandt and Michelangelo. There is so much I haven't discovered yet.

For our tenth anniversary, my husband and I walked slowly around the Metropolitan Museum of Art in New York City. I was stunned at the scale of the paintings. I had no idea how large many of them are. For example, Emanuel Leutze's *Washington Crossing the Delaware* fills an entire wall. The painting is 149 inches high by 255 inches long. (Or 12½ feet high by 21¼ feet long. It is so large that I imagined I could have jumped aboard if it wasn't so crowded already!) Everything about it was breathtaking.

I often wonder if the distractions in today's culture hamper kids from releasing untapped talent. Instead of being bored and going out to discover their talents, they are glued to TV and video games and the Internet. It takes an immense amount of time to create a masterpiece. Have our attention spans been compromised by social media? Are there artists in the world today who are doing what the artists of yesterday did? I don't know. I hope so.

Because it is this kind of art that showcases the glory of God. He's given us the gift of art because He loves us. I believe that art is an act of love. When my son draws me a picture, he is so excited to give it to me, not just so that I can see his talent, but because he loves me and wants me to take pleasure in it. This is what God does with us; He wants us to take pleasure in the beauty He's made and in the gifts He endows us with.

Furthermore we are His art. We are masterpieces that have been vandalized; we are torn and stained as we walk this earth, but He takes us and He makes us new again. I love seeing redemption in art. We are all filled with so much beauty, and oh how God wants to bring it out and use it for His Kingdom.

I can see the created and the fallen and the redemption in all of art; it all points to God's unfolding story. It's all God-inspired, whether we know it or not, because we are inspired by God.

I want to live my whole life seeking His face and embracing the art that He put inside of me and all around me. I want to know Him, my Artist, and paint with the color of my soul.

All of us can do this if we are willing to not be afraid.

As you seek Him, let Him seek you. He knows all there is, so there is nothing to fear. And you are filled with color and beauty, whether you know it or not. Beauty is in you because you are stamped with His image, and He is colorful and interesting.

Don't be afraid of your art.

And don't let your art be stolen by legalism or distraction or fear. You are beautiful.

French women have nothing on a woman who radiates the beauty of Jesus Christ.

✑ Unearthing Your Longings

What we wear on the inside of our souls is what is reflected to the world. What are you wearing? To be truly beautiful, spend time with the One who gives you beauty. When you seek Him with all your heart, you *will* shine. You will live as the beautiful woman He made you to be.

Go deeper by meditating on Psalm 27:8 and 1 Peter 3:3-4.

AN INVITATION TO PARIS!

It is said that French women are beautiful because they believe they are. This week, go through your closet and get rid of anything that doesn't make you feel good or lovely. Then indulge as much as your budget allows. Have you ever tried French milled soap or French lavender bubble bath or a French perfume? Have you worn a beret or come across a piece of jewelry with an Eiffel Tower charm? Add a touch of France to your beauty routine or accessories.

5

A NEW
DEFINITION
OF ROMANCE

WE ALL KNOW that Paris holds the title for most romantic city in the world. But, for me, in the fall of 2002, State College, Pennsylvania, had the chance to take the title when a very romantic *almost*-first kiss happened with my now husband.

It was a rainy day. We were at Penn State University's Movin' On festival on the HUB lawn. Mud was everywhere. Jesse, my "we're-not-dating-we're-just-friends-but-we-like-each-other"guy was visiting, and we just "so happened" to run into each other. We also happened to spend the whole afternoon together, listening to the different bands, sumo wrestling in inflatable costumes, jousting on a balance beam, and running around in the mud, as college students do. At one point during our running and flirting, I slipped and fell down, and he fell right on top of me.

My back was in the mud, and we were face-to-face. Our eyes were locked on each other, until he broke the stare and looked at my lips.

Here it comes; he's going to kiss me.

Suddenly, he got up. He chickened out! Can you believe it? It would have been a perfect first kiss. Instead he helped me up, awkwardness ensued, and we said our good-byes. I had to be somewhere that evening, but we promised we would try to catch up after. You know, as *just-friends* do.

To this day my husband and I still laugh about that moment and our almost-first kiss. But he says he didn't make the move because we weren't dating, and we were supposed to be praying about whether or not to date. Oh, yes, let me back up . . .

I met Jesse on a spring break trip to Memphis, Tennessee (this was before I moved there for the summer), with The Navigators collegiate ministry. His older sister, Renee, was a mentor of mine, and she is the one who invited him on the trip. Jesse was a freshman at a satellite campus of Penn State, and I was a junior at the main campus, three hours away.

Jesse played baseball and was supposed to travel with the team to Florida on spring break, but when that fell through, his sister invited him to come with us to Memphis. Which was a good thing, because he was on the fence spiritually, and a trip to Florida with the baseball team could have been very bad for him. You know, college baseball players and parties? Yeah, no.

Since he didn't have anything else lined up to do during spring break, he agreed to go.

The moment I saw him get out of the car, I said to Renee, "Your brother's really cute." I could tell by the look on her face what she was thinking: *Back off, Sarah*. She knew my tendency to jump into relationships. I was what you would call a serial monogamous dater. I would date a guy for around two years, and then we'd break up.

Jesse and I spent every day together on the trip, tutoring kids, fixing up the camp we were at, staying up late into the night talking. At the end of the week, he said to me, "I want you to know that I really like you."

I was flattered, and of course I had started to like him as well, but I said, "I can't date you. You're a freshman, and I'm a junior. You're beginning your college journey, and I'm almost done with mine." *I was so mature.*

We decided to take the rest of the school year and the summer to pray about whether or not we should date. This was probably his idea. So we didn't date, but we did promptly begin talking on the phone with each other regularly. It was somewhere during this time that the whole Movin' On almost-first kiss thing happened.

Then I moved to Memphis for the summer, and we decided not to talk and only to pray. For real this time.

It didn't take long for me to become lonely and desperate and dramatic over the summer, a less-than-ideal state of mind for what happened next. I started talking to my exboyfriend again. By the time I moved back to Pennsylvania, he was telling me he wanted to marry me. It only made sense in my mind to give it another try. So try we did. And then I got the phone call from Jesse. The one where we were supposed to talk about what we felt like the Lord had led us to decide about dating. Heh.

He started to talk first. "Sarah, I want to tell you . . ."

"Wait!" I said. "Let me go first."

This is like the part in the movie where you want to shout at the girl on screen to *shut up* and let the guy talk—but instead she stops him and she talks, and it's bad.

"No, no, let me talk first. I got back together with my ex this summer. I like you a lot, Jesse, but I think that you and I should just be friends. You feel the same way, right? I'm sorry I interrupted you. What were you going to say?"

He didn't feel the same way. He was about to tell me how much he cared for me, how he had been praying all summer, and how he knew that he wanted to be with me for the rest of his life.

But he didn't tell me that then. He hung up.

I know! I know, I know, I know. But I didn't know then!

The ex and I were together only for a little while longer when it became clear that we were a disaster together. I broke it off. I also finally realized that I should probably be single for a while. I needed to know how to be single and okay.

About a month after all this went down, I was on my computer when I saw Jesse's name on Instant Messenger. (Do you remember that?!) I decided to strike up a conversation.

Me: "Hey, are you coming to a Penn State game?"

Him: "No, I don't want to see you."

Subtle.

Me: "Aw, you should come to a game sometime."

I started harassing him in a teasing sort of way, until I finally realized: Jesse isn't even interested in talking to me. End of story. Or so I thought.

⤫

If you've never had the opportunity to attend a Penn State football game, let me tell you straight up it is not a game—it's an event. I always loved being a part of the enthusiastic crowd, one among thousands cheering for the home team. You can truly get lost in the crowd.

One fateful Saturday afternoon, I was standing on my dad's RV (for the awesome view) parked near the main walkway heading toward the stadium, and who should I spot walking in the midst of the masses?

"Jesse!" I yelled as loud as I could.

Somehow his friend heard me (I learned later) and said to Jesse, "Some crazy girl is screaming your name."

Jesse turned around, and I could tell by the look on his face that he wasn't glad to see me. But he walked over.

"Hi!" I said, trying to give him a hug.

And then I blurted out, "Oh, by the way, I broke up with my ex. But, you know, that's whatever."

He told me later that he was thinking, *Well, if it's whatever and doesn't mean anything, then why did you tell me?*

Total miscommunication again, which I missed.

"We should hang out," I said cheerily.

"No, I'm busy."

Ouch.

A few days later, on another IM chat, I convinced him to come up to hang with friends and catch up.

My persistence paid off, and he gave in. "Fine, I'll come see you."

So he and his friend came to visit, and we had such a fun time together. After he went back home to his campus, he called me and said, "I like you more than I did before, and I really want to date you."

I liked him, too, but I was still nervous about my guy issues (which were pretty clear with how this whole thing went down). "Listen," I said. "Because of everything that happened over the summer, let's go slow, because I don't want either of us to get hurt."

"That's fine," Jesse said, "but I want you to know that I'm pursuing you for marriage."

Nine months later we were married.

I'll tell you what really won me over. It was three things:

1. I had been told by a previous boyfriend that I didn't seem like someone who could ever be a mom. That really hurt my feelings because I wanted so bad to be a mom one day.

2. My mom and I had a difficult relationship, and often I would feel so confused and hurt after spending time with her (which wasn't often because she lived nearly 750 miles away).

3. I had always struggled with a passage from 1 Peter:

Don't be concerned about the outward beauty of fancy hairstyles, expensive jewelry, or beautiful clothes. You should clothe yourselves instead with the beauty that comes from within, the unfading beauty of a gentle and quiet spirit, *which is so precious to God.*
1 PETER 3:3-4, NLT (EMPHASIS ADDED)

A gentle and quiet spirit? I have always been loud and silly and gregarious, and I didn't know how to reconcile that Scripture with who I was.

How did Jesse win me over? By being a light to me in all those areas.

First, he told me, without any prompting, that he thought I would make a great mom one day. Of course I cried.

Next, we drove to Georgia so he could meet my mom. It didn't take long for things to escalate between my mom and me. She had been drinking, and at one point she started yelling at me and being hurtful. Jesse did something that no one had ever done for me before.

He stood up for me.

He literally got up on his feet and said in the most restrained and respectful way possible, "You will not talk to Sarah like this anymore." Then we left. We just got in the car and started driving back to Pennsylvania.

The last thing was straight from the Lord. I had never told Jesse about my struggle with the verses in 1 Peter; it was something I battled personally in my heart. In the spring of 2003, I was visiting him at his campus on the first day of spring break, and I had an inkling that he would ask me to marry him. We had talked about getting married, and I knew it was coming—I just didn't know exactly when he was going to pop the question. So, just to be prepared, I painted my nails red, his favorite color.

I spent the night in a friend's dorm room, and the next day Jesse called me and asked if we could go for a walk. He came to the dorm and off we went. It was a beautiful day.

He led me up through some woods to an area that overlooked the campus. He sort of nudged me ahead of him, and as I walked I saw something. On a large rock was an arrangement of flowers.

I turned around to say something, and there he was, on his knee with a ring in his hand.

"Will you marry me?"

"Yes!" I jumped into his arms, and we nearly fell over the side of the cliff. (It was a small cliff, but still.) He told me to look inside my ring because he had inscribed something there for me. It was 1 Peter 3:3-4. He told me that Scripture reminded him of me.

Jesse didn't know how much I needed that, but God knew. Crazy.

So we got married, and then we almost got divorced. I kid. Mostly.

We made the mistake of driving from Pennsylvania to Florida for our honeymoon. (I was afraid to fly because of 9/11 so I insisted that we drive.) My advice now? NEVER EVER attempt this when you're newly married.

Our first year in one word? *Rough.* So rough that on our first wedding anniversary, I wanted to do something special to make up for our hard times. Jesse was due home from work at five o'clock, so I prepared a candlelit dinner. I also donned my wedding dress as an added surprise. (Unfortunately, I couldn't zip it up.) Jesse was delayed at work for hours, so when he finally walked in the door, the candles had burned down to nubs. But when he saw me in my dress (I was facing him in order to hide the zipper problem), he fell to his knees and began to cry.

"You really love me?" he asked.

"Of course I do!"

He didn't know. He thought that because I was such a wretch much of that first year that I didn't love him.

Oh, but I did. It was a tough road in the years ahead, because marriage is this constant working out of two people coming together and figuring out how to stretch into this thing called love that isn't always romantic or happy or good. After three babies and the stuff of life, I felt like it was just too much.

Seven years in, *I* was done. I actually cried on the floor of my mother-in-law's laundry room telling her I couldn't do it anymore. She just listened and was so kind to me, saying she understood.

Bottom line? Marriage is hard. I mean, it's two sinners trying to walk through life together while occupying a shared space, where you have to see the other person every day. Even when you don't want to.

I always tell my kids, "Listen. You guys have to learn how to love each other because when you get married, at some point, your husband or wife is going to annoy you just like your brothers and sisters do now. And you're going to have to learn how to love and be kind and be friends with that person. Even though you didn't choose your siblings and you probably will choose your husband or wife, it doesn't matter. Everybody has quirks. Everybody has sin issues. Living with another human is hard. Period."

Sibling relationships, if stewarded toward love and friendship and grace, are such good preparation for marriage.

I've learned over the years that if hearts are tender, there's a settling in. My settling in with Jesse came at ten years. It came with an understanding of who we were, loads of grace in the midst of struggle so that shame and darkness didn't own us, letting go of outside pressure about what our marriage should look like, super honest discussions about hard things, and late nights with barbecued wings and a good movie. These are the keys that have helped Jesse and me get to where we are now—heading into our twelfth year together.

And I'm the happiest I've ever been.

A NEW DEFINITION OF ROMANCE

When I think of Paris, I think of strolls along the Seine, kisses in the moonlight, and extravagant dinners. The French are known for romance because they are known for their unabashed desire for pleasure. They want to enjoy every bit of life, so they take pleasure in all areas of it: food, drink, self-care, exercise, work, and romance.

But where did the idea of romance come from in the first place? As children, we were brought up on fairy tales with handsome princes falling in love with ordinary girls like us. When we were older, we wanted to wake up in Camelot with chivalrous knights proclaiming their undying love for us. In fact, that's the first definition of *romance* in Merriam-Webster: "a medieval tale based on legend, chivalric love and adventure, or the supernatural."

As I've thought more about the meaning of romance, I've come to my own conclusion: Above all else, romance is being rescued. It's being sought after and pursued, protected, cared for, loved—all of the things that God does for us. I believe that as women, we have the very desire for romance tucked inside of us. Everybody wants to be loved, but there's something in the soul of a woman that craves these specific aspects of romance. We want somebody to love us so much that he will risk everything to win us.

Isn't that exactly what God has done—and continues to do—for us? He has loved us to the point of His death. In my own life, I didn't go after God. He wooed me, vigilantly pursuing me over several years, without letting up.

It's what God continues to do with the church—you and me as believers—His bride. He rescues us. He protects us. He loves us. And one day after the final battle (and, yes, there's a dragon involved), He's going to bring us home. You and I are at the center of this epic romance story, being pursued and protected and longed for, and one day we're going to be taken home to our hero, Jesus. Real romance is laying your life down for someone, protecting that person, and putting him or her before yourself.

Just think of Hosea and Gomer. God tells Hosea to pursue and marry a prostitute, Gomer. She is an adulteress who has had children with other men, but God wants Hosea to keep pursuing her. This is what God does for each of us, even when we turn from Him and put other things or people before Him. He doesn't give up on us. As heartrending as the story of Hosea is, it's also a beautiful picture of what real romance is.

So you've been pursued and won by romance. What happens next?

This is where the rubber meets the road. Love, as described in the Bible, is not merely a lofty ideal but a hands-on experience.

Love is patient and kind. Love is not jealous or boastful or proud or rude. It does not demand its own way. It is not irritable, and it keeps no record of being wronged. It does not rejoice about injustice but rejoices whenever the truth wins out. Love never gives up, never loses faith, is always hopeful, and endures through every circumstance.

I CORINTHIANS 13:4-7, NLT

Did you catch the theme of sacrifice throughout those verses? The idea of thinking of the person you love above yourself?

Jesus sacrificed Himself because He loved us so much. It's all these choices that we make, and it's choosing to love. And it doesn't mean it's not accompanied with emotion. Of course it is. But emotion wanes. There's an ebb and a flow to emotion, to feeling. But there's always a choice to remain and to hope and to not give up and to be kind and to be patient and to endure through whatever circumstances threaten to destroy you.

My husband is romantic, not because he brings me flowers and jewelry (I prefer books anyway), but because he sets his own life aside for me. For two years straight, he gave up all his vacation days so I could travel to write and speak. And on Saturdays he gives me the day to write or do whatever I want to do.

In marriage, romance changes, looking a bit different over time. You see a need or sense a desire and act upon it. It's a practical sacrifice in the everyday things and finding ways to serve someone else. I let Jesse sleep in on Sunday mornings while I make a feast for the kids, and then he gets up. Or he brings me coffee and bacon in bed when I'm having a morning where I'm all *Everybody, stay away from me*. Or it's how we watch movies at night together. These are practical things. It's how he encourages me whenever I want to quit something, which is all the time. I get stressed out really easily, and whenever I want to quit, he'll say, "God called you to do this."

For Jesse and me, it's deeper and better and more beautiful than all the trappings of commercial ideas of love and romance. I would take our definition of romance over the romantic notion of Paris any day.

But I wouldn't turn down a trip to Paris with Jesse if it were offered. *Obviously.*

BRINGING PARIS INTO OUR EVERYDAY LIVES

If we went to Paris together, we'd get lost.

Intentionally.

We would have zero agenda, and we would just walk around. We would talk to strangers. We'd stop and eat whenever we smelled something delicious, an aroma wafting from a café or bakery. And we would take our time. If we saw some art, we'd linger in front of a painting. If we saw a great bookstore, we'd peruse for an hour or more, enjoying no set time to be anywhere or do anything. We're not the type of people who would follow a planned, down-to-the-minute schedule to see everything. We'd eventually see all the places we wanted to see, but it would be slow and deliberate.

But the reality is, we live in Lititz, Pennsylvania, not Paris. Where do we go, what do we see, how can we capture a sense of Paris here?

I'm learning to capture it in the seemingly insignificant moments.

For example, the other night my husband came home late from work. I was tired and the kids were sick, but I thought, *It's a moment.* I played a love song, and I walked over to him and snuck into his chest. He took my hand in his, put his arm around my waist, and we danced.

The kids giggled and tried to break in, but we just steadied ourselves together.

Later that night we argued about something, and life moved past the romance, but for that moment we brought Paris into our living room. And it was tender and lovely.

Paris is in the details. Taking my husband's hand when I could easily just be content without touching him. Choosing to kiss him a little longer than usual. Playing footsie with him at the movie theater or at dinner. Savoring the food when we're out, and laughing just a little too loud at his jokes. Letting him know that even though life and marriage can be frustrating as anything, it is still ours, and that matters.

Paris is taking the time to let imperfect love still matter.

And when we finally do go to Paris one day, we will enjoy

every walk, every dance, every hand-hold, every kiss, every footsie, and every bite of delectable food, just as we do at home.

Yeah, it's ugly sometimes in my house, and I'm selfish, and stretching into love with a sinner you have to sleep next to is such a crazy, ridiculous thing. But that crazy thing is God's idea, and so it matters.

So we celebrate.

We dance.

And once in a while, we even let the kids break in.

✌ *Unearthing Your Longings*

Romance is a beautiful thing when we remember what it really is about: sacrifice. The idea has its roots in chivalry, which is all about rescuing and protecting. It is not flowers and diamonds; it is a way of loving. When someone sacrifices for you because he or she loves you and knows you, it means something. Oh, how God loves and knows us! He is the most romantic person of all because He gave everything for us, sacrificing His very life.

Go deeper by meditating on Hosea 2:16, 19-20 and John 3:16.

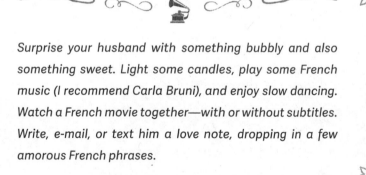

AN INVITATION TO PARIS!

Surprise your husband with something bubbly and also something sweet. Light some candles, play some French music (I recommend Carla Bruni), and enjoy slow dancing. Watch a French movie together—with or without subtitles. Write, e-mail, or text him a love note, dropping in a few amorous French phrases.

THE WONDER
OF IT ALL

(Striving to Mother Well)

My kids know I have a thing for Paris.

Every time they see an Eiffel Tower replica, they tell me about it. When they hear the French language, they shout, "Mom, DID YOU HEAR IT?" My son pretends to speak French to me, accent and all. My oldest daughter balks at any mention of Paris, acting like she doesn't like it. But it's in her soul, and because she has parts of me in her, she can't escape. And for some inexplicable reason, all of my kids were willing participants in the great croissant hunt.

I do love Paris, but I cherish my kids. Each one of them has been a unique treasure for Jesse and me. It's crazy to think how fast the time has gone . . .

Jesse and I weren't trying to get pregnant. We'd only been married for a little over a year, and he was still in school.

In fact, I had gone to the doctor's office twice to get on birth control, but both times I left empty-handed. I couldn't do it. I couldn't take the pills; it just didn't feel right. So we played that game where we paid attention to my body in order to not get pregnant. It worked for a year and a half.

I worked at a crisis pregnancy clinic, and one day I took one of the tests home. I didn't think I was pregnant; I had no reason to believe I was. I just . . . wanted it. Somewhere in my heart, I longed to be pregnant. It wasn't a good time, of course; my husband was still in school, we lived in a tiny apartment, and we were barely scraping by. But there was still that longing.

I took the test, and as I watched it, I saw that it was going to show that I wasn't pregnant. I started to cry.

But then that line turned into two lines, and there it was—the sign of new life. My hands started to shake, and I got butterflies in my tummy, and I thought, *Is this real?* I called the doctor and asked if I could come in for a blood test so I could know for sure.

The blood test confirmed that it was true.

I was all smiles, all wonder and joy.

That night as Jesse and I were getting into bed, I just kept smiling. He cuddled close to me, and I put the pregnancy test on the pillow next to him. He looked at it and thought it was a joke. He thought I took it from the clinic and that it belonged to someone else.

I just kept smiling.

And then he smiled, because he knew.

For three months I was sick. I was in bed or on my couch most days. I couldn't keep anything down, and at one point I had to go to the hospital for an IV because I was dehydrated. It was awful.

But that little one was growing safely in me, and that was magical to me.

❧

My water broke in the middle of the night, a rushing release; it was time. I had prepared for this. My husband and I had taken three months of birthing classes so we could have a med-free childbirth.

I gathered up my Gatorade and snacks, and we drove to the hospital. I was having contractions every few minutes.

I refused the wheelchair because I wanted to walk this baby out of me.

I threw up.

No snacks.

I decided to get into the Jacuzzi. Ah yes, that was what I needed.

Concentrate, breathe. *Oh, God, it hurts.*

Transition.

Push!

Two hours of sweating and screaming and pushing and then . . .

She was born. My beautiful Ella was out of me and in the world, and all of life was about to change.

I couldn't hold her though. I was shaking and exhausted and hot and cold. Jesse took her.

After a few minutes, the nurse placed her gently on my chest, and I held her close and cried. She was a wonder, and I was in awe.

Over the next few days I would stare at her and think, *How could anyone not believe in God?* Life is so incredible.

Each phase of her growth was lovely to me. Watching her discover something new, or say a word, or crawl, or giggle was all so fascinating to me. She was this little human who needed me, but who was going to grow into her own person with thoughts and opinions and a personality all her own. Who would she be? What was inside of her? What color had God put into her very soul? The fact that I had a front-row seat to this human's life was wild to me.

Within the next few years, two more new lives came along, and with each one I was completely and utterly amazed. I was tired all the time, and being responsible for three little ones was tough, but there was still the wonder of it all. I was responsible for taking care of these precious ones, making sure to nurture them and teach them about the world and give them what they needed to be healthy and loved. It's a serious thing to raise a life.

Welcome to the world, little humans; I am your guide.

I will show you how to navigate this great big, wondrous, sometimes-overwhelming world. I will do my best, but I'm still walking through it and figuring it out, as well. At least we're in it together.

⌒♉

Parenting is a crazy thing, isn't it? While trying not to lose our minds in the responsibility and sleeplessness of it all, we are also the ones who are teaching and training and helping our little people understand and be somewhat healthy in this world, adding beauty to it, making it a better place. We are not taught how to do this, at least most of us aren't. I don't remember taking any Raising Humans 101 classes, do you?

And even if there were, this raising of intricate souls who have their own bents and colors and gifts and sin is complicated. How do I do this parenting thing well, when most of the time I'm faltering at my own life?

But I'll tell you, I long to give this parenting role my best—understanding that my best will often be a bit of a mess, but at least I will try. I will give myself to the work, to the season, and I will—I can only—surrender myself to the Lord and ask for His grace as I learn to parent in a good way.

Dear Lord, help us all.

There are days when I feel so out of control with parenting. It can be overwhelming thinking about my responsibility to raise my children so that they can navigate life and in turn be life-givers to the world. I not only want them to know about the God who made them, loves them, and has a purpose for their time on this earth; I want them to be productive human beings—giving, serving, loving, and communicating intelligently with others. I want to prepare them for surviving in a sin-infested world. I want them to be Kingdom-bearers and influencers for good.

The fact is, there is a ton of beauty and goodness in the world and in people, but there is also darkness. I want my children to be light; my hope is that they will know and love the Father and then know and love others. But even if they never make a personal commitment to Him, I still want to have the assurance that I invested my life in caring for and building good things into their hearts, minds, and souls so they can live well—so they can live fully. As much as I believe that they will never live full lives without them knowing the One who places the fullness of light and life in us, I want them to know I love them no matter what.

There is nothing they could do or say that would make me love them more or make me love them less. Could I be disappointed or even brokenhearted over choices they may make? Of course. But they are my babies, and they always will be. It's my job—my opportunity—to love them, honor them, and nurture these individuals whom God made them to be. It's not about my agenda for their lives; it's looking deep into them, discovering who they are and where they shine, and helping to pull their gifts out and develop them.

What a joy it is to help a fellow human being uncover and help cultivate his or her potential.

THAT TIME I QUIT

I was in Colorado for a conference, where I was a speaker.

I had already given my talk, and after a long and fun day, I crashed into bed and fell into a deep sleep. But in the middle of the night I was startled awake by a crushing dream. In my dream I yelled at one of my daughters and watched her walk away, and there was this terrible feeling that I had lost her, and that it was too late to get her back. The weight of regret that gripped me was one of the most strikingly painful feelings I have ever had—I could hardly breathe. I felt as if I had actually lost my daughter forever. The dream terrified me, because I knew it was a revelation of what could come to pass if I didn't stop and invest more of myself into my children's lives. I would lose precious years with my children, and I would deeply regret my choices.

That dream woke me up.

I had a choice to make. I could keep going in the direction I was going—doing too much, focusing on writing and speaking and being at the mercy of deadlines—or I could quit for a while, get centered, and catch the years.

I didn't want to be double-minded anymore. I needed to make a clean break if I was going to avoid any regrets.

Here is a journal entry I wrote after having the dream:

I have to make a clean break and experience the hidden years before it's too late. I have only ten years before Ella is eighteen. That's it, ten years. I'm sick over it. So Ella will be at the forefront of my mind when I quit. . . . I know God will go before me, and it will be okay. The pain of quitting and facing people in light of my decision is better than the pain of regret.

I'm not going to regret my life. I'm scared, but I'm resolved.

This was the Scripture that came to me after I decided to quit:

> *The Lord GOD has opened My ear;*
> *And I was not disobedient*
> *Nor did I turn back.*
> *I gave My back to those who strike Me,*
> *And My cheeks to those who pluck out the beard;*
> *I did not cover My face from humiliation and spitting.*
> *For the Lord GOD helps Me,*
> *Therefore, I am not disgraced;*
> *Therefore, I have set My face like flint,*
> *And I know that I will not be ashamed.*
>
> ISAIAH 50:5-7

I committed that day to taking a full year off.

A year off from blogging, speaking, and other public ministry. I determined to set my face like flint to get my priorities straight and get my home in order. I became resolved to give myself to the season of motherhood, to take care of my home, and to invest in my community. I decided to set benchmarks for myself, and after the year was up, begin writing publicly again if those benchmarks were consistently (not perfectly) in place.

Writing and blogging and speaking were not my problem; my double mind was. "If a house is divided against itself, that house cannot stand" (Mark 3:25, NIV), and I want a sturdy home. For out of a sturdy home comes peace, rest, good works, hospitality, and light.

I don't believe in making an idol out of home or family, but I do know that stability and intention and time-giving love are at the forefront of healthy people who can go into the world and serve it well. And while I know there are no guarantees for how my children will turn out, or what they will choose for their lives, I know that I will be able to look back knowing I did my best to steward their souls.

I don't carry the weight of their salvation or their choices, but I do carry the weight of my job in teaching them, building beautiful memories with them, and preparing them for life.

Thankfully, we don't carry this weight alone.

OH, I THOUGHT YOU WERE DISCIPLINED

Every time I feel exasperated by my children, I think of Proverbs 29:17, "Correct your son, and he will give you comfort; He will also delight your soul." Oh yes, I am to show them the way and help them to be civilized, and from this I will benefit too.

Well, I was clued in not too long ago that I had some work cut out for me. I had clearly been slipping in my parental duties. Here's what happened . . .

I swooshed into the church office with a flourish, myself and my three tagalongs.

We were meeting with one of the pastors because two of my children were preparing to get baptized.

The wonderful secretary got me some coffee so I could be fully awake for this important meeting.

We walked into the cozy room with comfy chairs and a desk, and I told my youngest to have a seat and start coloring. I had prepared in advance, making sure I was equipped so my littlest had something to do while the pastor talked to my older two. I had even laid down the ground rules before we entered the building: "No running around; no yelling; use your manners; listen to Mommy."

I've got this.

But no sooner did we sit down and the pastor started talking to my son when my five-year-old (the one who was supposed to be coloring) got up and started walking around the room.

"Honey, sit down and color. Remember what we talked about?"

No go.

She proceeded to sit on the couch. Then she slumped on the couch. Then she started bouncing on the couch.

I pulled her aside and talked to her quietly, noticing out of the corner of my eye that my son was slouching now and not paying attention.

My little one started asking the pastor random questions. He pulled out a toy to entertain her, which of course her brother wanted to play with.

Before I knew it, self-control went out the window. *What happened? I was prepared! Why didn't they listen?* I was so embarrassed.

We wrapped up the painful meeting and headed to the car. I was so angry at their disrespectful behavior. I was angry because I thought I had them trained in how to behave in that type of setting. Boy, was I wrong, and it was cold water in my face!

I tried calling Sally Clarkson, my friend and mentor. No answer. I called another friend, Soleil, who happens to be one of the kindest, most gracious, wisest women I know.

She answered.

"Soleil, it's Sarah. I am so angry with how my kids behaved, and I'm not sure what to do now, after the fact."

"Tell me what happened," Soleil said.

I recounted the morning's fiasco. She listened, and then she said, "I will come alongside you and work with you and support you."

Soleil has five children, ranging from three months to ten

years, and she is a great mom. I have watched her parent and have always been inspired by her.

One of the first things she encouraged me to do was to let myself off the hook. "Take the rest of the day and focus completely on your children," she advised. "Observe them, identifying and writing down any frustrating issues that arise, and how those issues make you feel. Then we'll talk tomorrow."

When we got home, I did what Soleil said. I really paid attention to my children's actions and responses. And that's when I noticed it.

My children obey me, but strictly on their terms, rather than following exactly what I ask.

For example, one of my children was on their bike and I asked them to come up the drive and put it away. This child took their sweet time, going past the driveway and circling in a neighbor's driveway, before putting the bike away.

I couldn't believe it.

Now listen, I don't expect perfect obedience, and I know that training and maturing is a process . . . a lifetime process. But I need my children to respect me. I need my children to honor and obey me because I am their mother and God has given me the authority to mother.

If they can't honor and obey me, how will they honor and obey God? How will they love and respect others if they don't learn it first at home?

I was ready to get to work.

IDENTIFYING THE ISSUES

Here are the steps I took after my conversation with Soleil:

1. Observe the frustrating issues and write them down for each child
2. Pay attention to what I'm feeling when those issues arise
3. Learn how to discipline lovingly
4. Be consistent
5. Note progress

Issues:

Child—lack of focus/follow-through
Child—disobedience, disrespect (argues when asked to do something or not do something, takes his or her time)
Child—whines, drags feet

Ways to deal:

- Talk with a friend who has gone before me and has well-behaved kiddos
- Talk with each of my kiddos one-on-one about issues to work on
- Learn parenting skills alongside other friends
- Spend time loving my kids in specific ways that make them feel loved (get their hearts!)

This is definitely a work in progress, but I can tell you what has taken place so far.

I have put in place three things in order to appropriately and lovingly train my children:

1. I have decided to give each of my children a love language test so I can make sure to love them the way they feel loved.
2. I have decided to join with Soleil as she has invited myself and some other friends to go through a parenting course with her.
3. I have been doing my best to nip wrong behaviors in the bud!

PINPOINTING MY KIDS' LOVE LANGUAGE

I have been with my children long enough to know how they feel loved, but I still thought it would be fun to have them take a love language profile test.[12]

The results? For my youngest daughter, the test indicated quality time; for my son, gifts; and for my oldest daughter, it said words of affirmation.

I also implemented a suggestion from my sister-in-law, something she had heard: Ask your children how mommies and daddies love their children.

I asked each of my children this question separately.

My oldest child said, "By giving them special things." *Huh.* I thought she liked quality time. I guess she likes both.

My son said, "Taking them special places." Knowing his personality, I had always pegged his love language to be physical touch, but it was enlightening to see that he enjoys quality time as well.

The youngest said, "Giving them hugs and cuddles." Let's just say, I was surprised once again.

Okay then, I thought, *I am going to love these kids into obedience!*

First up, my oldest daughter.

She and I have implemented a secret girls night once a month, where I rent a movie online, we go out and get a treat, and we watch our movie when everybody is in bed. She loves this, and so do I.

She often asks, "When are we going to do our girls night, Mom?"

Jesse jokes that he's going to come home from work one night and there's going to be platters of food all over the bed, and we'll be watching our movie. I love it.

At some point I will do this with my other kiddos as well.

Another thing I have started doing with my oldest is writing her a letter once a month, and she writes me back. I want her to have words from me that she can look back on and keep, words of encouragement and love from her mama. I would share a letter in this book, but it's special between the two of us.

As I mentioned above, my son's love languages are gifts, physical touch, and quality time.

Every morning, without fail, he comes to my room, tucks himself into bed next to me, and proceeds to sniff my face, all the way up my cheek. If I've already showered, he cries; he likes my natural smell, my "pheromones." I make sure to give him lots of cuddles.

And my youngest, she really likes to cuddle too. She wants to curl up with me and stay put. She's very tender and very sweet. She is always asking to go on dates, so Jesse and I try to make time to take her out.

I will love these babes and make our relationship a priority, I will learn to parent the best I can, and I will give myself to the work.

Oh, and when we get to Paris, I know exactly what each of them would want to do there.

Ella would want to go where all the food is—cafés and bakeries. She takes after me in that way.

My son, Caed, would want to see a concert or a show. He loves music, dancing, and plays.

And Caroline would want to go to all the shops and see all the pretty clothes and shoes and makeup. She'd want to find some makeup that I would let her put on. She always wants to look pretty. She wants to change a couple of times a day into different dresses. I'm sure that would not be a problem in one of the fashion capitals of the world.

IMPRINTING A SOUL

"It is a personal relationship with a real person whose soul is alive in which the deepest imprints of life are given."
SALLY CLARKSON

Here is a piece I wrote on my blog in March 2013 that really resonated with readers:

> My oldest came to my room after bedtime and said, "Caroline keeps saying she needs you."
>
> I went upstairs and looked at my sweet little one, who is now four, curled up under her covers peacefully. I said, "Do you need me?" She nodded. I knelt down, crawled into bed with her, and snuggled up close. "Lullaby, and goodnight . . ." I began to sing softly. I rubbed her head and nuzzled my nose into her hair, and felt the delicateness of her soft skin. She lay there precious and still, with heavy eyelids, and I kissed her head and thought, *How many times have I rushed bedtime? How many moments like this have I lost?*
>
> And it was there in her bed in that quiet moment that I realized how much she needed me, and how much I had neglected that need.
>
> When my straggly-haired hippie girl was only two-years old, I did everything I could to get her to go to bed, but she wouldn't stay put. Sometimes she would get out of bed twenty times, and just about every time she would say, "I just want to be with you."
>
> I thought she was disobeying, and I felt like I was going crazy because I was *so* tired. I just wanted my own time; *I needed a break.* So after trying all sorts of discipline techniques and after crying and

praying, I would sometimes get angry and take it out on that little girl who was just trying to figure out how to be with her mama. Because that's what it was about. She just needed me to be *with* her. And all my fighting against it did nothing but cause pain and tears and regret.

I know this now, and so here is what I have to say to all you tired mamas out there:

I know you're about worn-out, and most days, bedtime can't come soon enough. You need a break or you feel like you will lose. your. mind. But let me tell you, it hurts to lie down next to your baby and realize just how much you missed the ball when it came to her needs. It hurts when you remember how you thought you needed to discipline her when really, she just needed you to lie down and cuddle and comfort.

Do you remember when you were little and how you wanted your mom or dad to stay with you just a *little* while longer? Do you remember ever having your head rubbed and how good that felt? Did you ever get sung to?

I'm telling you, friend, sometimes we need to just quit fighting and give in. I know there are nights you just can't give anything else, and that's okay. But on the nights you can push through just a little more, do it. Sing to your two-year-old; snuggle down close in their bed; rub their head; nuzzle into their hair; and whisper, "You are a delight" (even if you don't feel it).

"You can go now, Mama," Caroline says.

I smile, roll off her bed, and quietly leave her room. She got her fill, and now she can sleep. Oh that girl, the wild one, she is *truly* a delight. I whispered those words to her so many times, praying that they would eventually be true, and now, without a doubt, they are 100 percent true. She is an utter joy to me.

She just needed to grow up a little bit.

And honestly, so did I.

Because what I know now that I didn't know then, was that she just wanted me. Just how God made it so—a little one to want, to need her mama.

That article was shared more than a million times. Why? Because we know that our little ones need us; those precious, eternal souls in our care need our comforting, our time, our words, our kisses, and our cuddles. They need to be nurtured. And not only on a physical level—their very souls need cultivating. It is my job and my joy as a mother to have the responsibility to nurture my child's soul.

WHAT DOES IT MEAN TO NURTURE A SOUL?

Nurturing a soul means paying attention to it—the details, the nuances, the bents, the beauty. The souls of our children have been woven by God into a unique and fascinating personhood. The first way we as mothers can nurture a soul is to observe it and be conscientious toward it.

The parents who devote time to their children
even when it is not demanded by glaring misdeeds
will perceive in them subtle needs for discipline,
to which they will respond with gentle urging or
reprimand or structure or praise, administered
with thoughtfulness and care. They will observe
how their children eat cake, how they study, when
they tell subtle falsehoods, when they run away
from problems rather than face them. They will
take the time to make these minor corrections and
adjustments, listening to their children, responding
to them, tightening a little here, loosening a little
there, giving them little lectures, little stories, little
hugs and kisses, little admonishments, little pats
on the back.[13]

In order to nurture our children's souls, we must become
intentional about filling them with good things. I want to
fill my children with rich stories, testimonies of saints, good
music, art, delicious food, and deep relationships with good
friends. One of the ways we do this is by having a daily
teatime, where I read out loud to my kids. We also look at
beautiful paintings from an art book I have and try to paint
them. We read biographies and interesting literature, such
as *White Fang* and *The Hobbit*. We listen to different genres
of music, from classical to rap. (My husband has a thing for
Christian rapper Lecrae.)

I like how Clay Clarkson puts it:

We cultivate the soil of our children's hearts with the nutrients that will allow spiritual qualities to grow there—the language of God's truth, the behaviors of the Christian life, the reality of God. In essence, we familiarize our children with the ways and words of the kingdom of God so that when they accept the gospel of salvation, it will be a natural step forward rather than a radical change of direction. We are readying their hearts, preparing fertile soil so that the gospel can sink deep roots into their lives. When the gospel takes hold, they will be saved from their sins and given a new spirit. Then the Holy Spirit will begin the lifelong process of producing the character of Christ in them.[14]

I have found that in order to make space in my children's souls for the beautiful things, the holy things, I first need to be aware of how they're spending their time and what is going into their minds.

WHAT I LEARNED FROM BEETHOVEN

I was driving to the library with my kiddos, and I put in a tape about Beethoven: stories from his life accompanied by selections of his music throughout. We were all enjoying it. As I listened, questions began popping into my head: *If Beethoven had had a TV, would he have realized his musical gift at such a young age . . . or even at all? Would his compositions have been as brilliant if he had written them during a commercial break? I wonder how many children in my kids' generation will never fulfill or discover their potentials because they are too "busy" watching TV or playing video games? How many gifts are being missed because kids aren't "bored" enough to tinker and explore and think and create?*

If there were TVs and video games in the time of some of the great composers and artists of yesteryear, would they have produced the beautiful, life-enriching art that we have today?

According to the American Academy of Pediatrics (AAP),

Studies have shown that excessive media use can lead to attention problems, school difficulties, sleep and eating disorders, and obesity. In addition, the Internet and cell phones can provide platforms for illicit and risky behaviors.

Their recommendation?

Television and other entertainment media should be avoided for infants and children under age two. A child's brain develops rapidly during these first years, and young children learn best by interacting with people, not screens.[15]

In a separate AAP article, Dr. David L. Hill confirms that this early and extensive exposure to "screen time" can cause serious damage to children and should not be taken lightly by parents.

> Good evidence suggests that screen viewing
> before age two has lasting negative effects on
> children's language development, reading skills, and
> short-term memory. It also contributes to problems
> with sleep and attention. If "you are what you eat,"
> then the brain is what it experiences, and video
> entertainment is like mental junk food for babies
> and toddlers.[16]

I appreciated this research on screen time and kids. It confirmed what was playing out in front of me with my own three. My kids would get whinier with the more TV they watched. They would get more demanding as well. And, of course, the more time they spent in front of the TV, the less time they had to read books and do anything using their imaginations.

No more! I decided that we would go one week with no TV except for our Friday night family movie night. I wanted to watch how my children behaved during this TV fast and how it affected our family overall.

Once again, I prepared in advance. First, I let my children know what was going to happen. I wasn't going to surprise them. I then made sure we had enough markers and crayons and paper and coloring books on hand.

Ya'll, I was nervous. What if I needed a break? What if I went crazy? What if I ran out of things for them to do?

Side note: I homeschool my children, so they're with me *all* day, every day. Days can get suffocating. TV can provide temporary relief for everyone on the hard days.

I was determined though. I wanted better for my children. So how did it turn out?

Wonderfully.

My oldest, who was eight at the time, never even asked to watch TV. I think my son asked once at the beginning of the week, and my four-year-old asked twice. That's it. They did puzzles, played with each other by using their imaginations, colored, had friends over, and listened while I read to them. They were fine.

I was fine.

And I liked it. I liked knowing my kids were using their minds and enjoying life without the screen. No computers, no iPads or game systems, just relationships and imagination. It was all good.

But . . .

I didn't want to get rid of the TV permanently. That seemed . . . well, crazy. However, Jesse was all for it. "Let's do it."

I wasn't ready. Even though I liked the results I was seeing in the kids, I couldn't commit to *forever* (or something like that).

So we went back to watching TV because it was easy and accessible.

It wasn't long before I noticed it was becoming a crutch, so drastic measures were needed. We pulled the plug and gave it away.

I am determined to see my kids use their imaginations and while doing so discover their unexplored talents. I want them to be bored. I want to get uncomfortable so I can invest more into them. And it's not so bad having a game night instead of a movie night.

Because . . .

What if?

I really want to preserve childhood for my children so that they have memories and imagination and so that they've experienced life and the world around them.

> May they not grow up to imitate addiction to the computer. May they not learn and display passivity from adults ignoring their needs while paying too much attention to Facebook, Twitter, blogs, and cell phones. May they not copy the habit of observing parents dwelling hour after hour in front of impersonal machines, while neglecting to honor and invest in real-time relationships. . . .
>
> May all children be blessed with the gift of play, imagination, free time, and the space to be outdoors to explore. May they wonder at the marvels of God's creation. May they have the treasure of real human beings who hold their hands while exploring the world, or who rock them to sleep and sing them

real songs or scratch their backs at bedtime and tell them their own love stories. And may they daily hear the words of their creator God, and marvel at His excellence and grow to love Him with all of their hearts.[17]

LIGHTENING MY LOAD *(by Lightening Theirs)*

If my family and I are going to move to Paris one day and live there for a year (oh, did I not mention that before?), we're going to have to get used to having less stuff. Plus, if I'm going to mother well, I'm going to have to be a sane person, and messy rooms make me crazy. In an effort to get my family on that track, I did what any rational mother would do.

I went into my kids' rooms and told them they had to get rid of everything, except for twenty things.

I'm not a pack rat. I'm not one of those parents who keeps tons of things. This should be easy. Surely, my children don't have more than twenty-five or thirty things.

I was shocked.

My kids probably had a hundred things among all three of them. You forget about all the little things you get for them, the dollar items you pick up without even thinking twice.

They had picked out twenty things but there were still so many things left, and it was hard for them to decide what to give away. This is why kids have a hard time cleaning their rooms—because there's so much stuff all over the place, and they get discouraged just looking at it.

I didn't want my kids to be overwhelmed, and I didn't want to be overwhelmed. So we pared down together and *voilá!* We were all happier.

THANK GOD FOR CHILDREN

My girls and I were walking through Target, me going a little too fast and them trying to keep up with me, when I heard my five-year-old say in the perkiest voice, "Oh, I see you lost a tooth!"

I turned around and *oh my.* She was talking to a grown man.

He looked at me and smiled, only one front tooth visible, and said, "I forgot to put in my dentures."

I mean. So funny.

This is what children do: They bring laughter to our world. They are curious and observant and innocent in their understanding of so many things. They make us remember, for a moment, what it is like to see the world with fresh eyes and unscathed hearts.

They don't have scars yet. Life is truly wondrous to them.

It is their wonder that helps me not only become a better mother, but a better human. I slow down, and my scars soften; when you stop and look, there is so much around us to be fascinated by.

Most days, I am rushing. "Come on! Get your shoes on. Hurry up!"

There is always one child who lags behind the others because that small person has stopped to examine a leaf or inspect an intriguing bug. Have I paid attention to the simple things that thrill my kids—the different shapes and colors of leaves or how big a cicada's eyes are or how loud a chorus of these insects can be? It might be the first time they've ever seen that color of leaf or that type of bug. What if I got down and we looked together?

"Look at that interesting shape and the bright color God gifted it with."

We can choose to just see, or we can see and experience.

This is life, seeing and experiencing what God has given us.

I can mother well when I remember to put myself into the shoes of a child. I am more compassionate, more wide-awake, and more aware.

In their book *Raising Kids with Character That Lasts*, John and Susan Alexander Yates give a wonderful illustration of why we can't let our kids grow up without us—there is so much to enjoy.

> We will never "arrive" in family life. When I was surrounded with small children, I thought, *If I can just hang on until they are older, I can relax.* It was as if I viewed life as a ladder rather than a garden. I was always struggling to get to the next rung, the next season in life. So focused would I become on simply

making it to the next age that I often missed out on the blessings of the moment. And at the next age, more challenges were waiting. There were different character traits to work on and new circumstances in my own life that revealed weaknesses. Would I ever "get to the top"?

Life is not a ladder to climb but a garden to enjoy. The gardener's joy is in his work, a job that is never finished. He delights in the process of the work. Our work in families is never finished. We will never perfect character, nor will our children. We are people in process. Yet there is joy in the process if we relax, knowing that the blessing is in the journey rather than in the completion of the job. When we relax, the atmosphere of our homes will become less tense and more joyful and we will rely more on the power of the Master Gardener.[18]

❧ *Unearthing Your Longings*

I know you want to mother well, but sometimes that mother well is dry. You are tired, and you can't handle doing one more thing right now. That's okay. Rest and fill your well. For you who are ready for more, think about the vision you have for mothering. What do you want to build into your children? Where can you start? Is there anything you need to say no to in order to have the energy for your family? What are your children's love languages? How can you practically love each one of them well? You were made to mother, and you can do this. One step at a time, in the holy grace of your heavenly Father.

Go deeper by meditating on Isaiah 40:11 and Luke 14:28.

AN INVITATION TO PARIS!

Let your children experience the delight of Paris! Surprise them with a special pastry, teach them a French song like "Frère Jacques" or "Alouette," draw an Eiffel Tower on paper or build one out of whatever's on hand, let them paint a replica of a French master's artwork, print out a Monet picture for them, or find a discounted calendar that features paintings each month. Don't forget to join in!

HOLY DNA

For you have died and your life is hidden with Christ in God.

COLOSSIANS 3:3

EVERY PLACE HAS its own DNA, you could say.

Here in Lititz, the DNA consists of old-town charm, the scent of chocolate in the air from the Wilbur Chocolate factory, and the pride of being named the "coolest small town in America."

The DNA of Paris is romance and pleasure, of course.

The DNA of my soul is holiness.

My soul, because it is infused with the Holy Spirit, is sacred ground. But while it was created as sacred, it has been marred. And for a while all I knew was the marring, the ugly.

Until He showed me just how beautiful I could be.

❧

The room was full of old things.

Around me, in an old barn converted into a retreat center, the walls were covered with buckets and farming tools and all sorts of things that would clang loudly if they fell. There were shabby, torn couches scattered throughout the room and folding chairs occupied by college students, including me.

The speaker asked, "What would you do if Jesus walked into the room right now?"

I would hide, I thought. *I would hide from Him because He's good and beautiful, and I'm bad and ugly. I would hide in the corner, behind one of these worn couches, bent down, with my face on my knees. I wouldn't want Jesus to see me.*

I was filled with shame.

After a few minutes, either through the speaker's words or God's Spirit encouraging me, I suddenly had a great peace that I didn't have to hide. In fact, if Jesus walked into the room, I was certain He would come over to me and hug me and put His hands on my face and call me daughter. It didn't matter that He knew everything about me right then, from my past, and for all of the future. He *knew* me, and He loved me just the same. That was the first time I knew I was loved and that I was His. I could hide myself in Him; I could tuck in, and He would take over—if I let Him. He could have all of me, and I could have all of Him.

That is identity.

It is being so enveloped by Christ, and Him by you, that you become the same; you can identify with Him because He is so close to you and vice versa. This is why we must remain in Him if we are to stay secure in our identity. After all, *identity* means *sameness*.

WE ARE MADE TO KNOW WHO WE ARE

I heard someone say once that if you don't figure out your identity in your twenties, you are likely to have a midlife crisis in your fifties. This makes complete sense to me. *We are made to know who we are.*

As I mentioned earlier, French women are known for accepting who they are, embracing it, and working to grow into it. They don't strive to be like someone else; they want to be fully themselves.

I think French women are on to something.

When God wove us together out of dust and love, it was personal and intimate. God did not speak me into existence like He did the sun and the moon and the plants and the animals. He *formed* me, molding me with His hands, and He breathed His breath of life into me. He knit me together in my mother's womb. He knows me by name, and He knows every hair on my head. I am not spoken into being. I am created. I am art. I am the artwork of God.

But that intimate relationship between God and man didn't end at creation. One of my favorite stories of Jesus healing someone is recorded in the Gospel of John. As Jesus was walking along, He saw a blind man, and this is what he did:

> *He spat on the ground, and made clay of the spittle,*
> *and applied the clay to his eyes, and said to him, "Go,*
> *wash in the pool of Siloam" (which is translated, Sent).*
> *So he went away and washed, and came back seeing.*
>
> JOHN 9:6-7

Now at first, this action seems kind of gross and unnecessary. Jesus could have just proclaimed that the man was healed and he would have been. But spit? Eeww. But then I remember how God made man in the first place.

"Then the LORD God formed the man from the dust of the ground" (Genesis 2:7, NLT). It was as if Jesus was forming new eyes for the blind man, from the very dust which he came from. But it wasn't just the dust or the mud; Jesus *touched him.* He gently put the mud over the man's eyes, and it was personal and tender.

Our bents, our personalities, and our skill sets are not accidents. God put them into us for His glory and purposes. To not accept how God made us would be to deny His glory.

When we are fully ourselves, He is fully glorified.

This is why it is so important to accept who you are, to push out voices of opposition, and to walk free and confidently in God. We do not love ourselves as much as we love how God lovingly, personally created us.

I love who I am because I was made with love. And I want to be fully me so that my God can be fully glorified.

THE DNA OF HOLINESS

The first thing you need to get straight is knowing where you stand before God, and there are only two places: unrighteous or righteous.

You are either His child, and therefore bear His righteous DNA through Christ, or you are not.

If you are His, oh friend, know this and take it in deep: You are perfect right now according to heaven. You are complete because of Christ. Hebrews 10:14 says, "For by a single offering he has perfected for all time those who are being sanctified" (ESV). And this, from 2 Corinthians 5:21: "He made Him who knew no sin to be sin on our behalf, so that we might become the righteousness of God in Him."

Author and pastor John Lynch describes it like this:

> If I brought a caterpillar to a biologist and asked
> him to analyze and describe its DNA, he'd say,
> "John, I know it looks like a caterpillar to you, but
> scientifically, in every testable DNA result, this is
> fully and completely a butterfly." Wow! God has
> wired into a creature looking nothing like a butterfly,
> a complete perfect butterfly identity. And because
> the caterpillar is a butterfly in essence, it will one day
> display the behaviors and attitudes and attributes

of a butterfly. The caterpillar matures into what is already true about it. In the meantime, berating the caterpillar for not being more like a butterfly will probably just hurt its little ears. And so it is with us. God has given us the DNA of godliness. We are saints, we are righteous, and nothing we can do will make us more godly than we already are. God knows our DNA. He knows we're Christ in me, and now He's asking us to join Him in what He already knows is true.[19]

We are caterpillars on the outside, but inside, according to heaven and because of Christ, we are butterflies! Doesn't that just make you smile?

If you know Him, you are already *changed*. Now you are just maturing into who you already are.

THE MOLDING

We are clay.

Can clay mold itself? Of course not. Clay needs hands to grab its lumpiness and knead it, smooth it, shape it, and give it purpose.

We cannot mold ourselves.

We keep failing, and we have so many weaknesses, and we can't seem to get it together no matter how much we try or pray. It's been so many years and we still don't get things right, and we think, *God, You haven't conquered these things in me yet.* We strive and strive when we go on our own. We think, *I'm just going to try harder; I'm going to do better, I'll be better.* And then when we fail, we fall really hard, and we teeter on this line of grace and shame, and it's easy to fall on the shame side. *I'm never going to change; what is wrong with me?* But if we remember that we are clay and God is the Potter, then we know we cannot make this clay into whatever we want; we cannot mold ourselves no matter how hard we try.

He is the only one who can mold us.

So we say to Him, "Take this lump of clay, my weaknesses and failures. I can't do it. I can't form myself. I lie down trying."

Accept and utilize the Holy Spirit in you, and the grace to get up and keep going when you fall down. Don't take your eyes off of Him.

God provides power and grace, and He will work in our lives to complete the purposes He has laid out for us before the foundation of the earth. Not even our sin can thwart our holy DNA. I am in my Father's will; His will be done, no matter what. No matter my weakness. I can walk confidently because of His power in me. How easily I forget about the Holy Spirit!

It's easy to feel self-pity, to get down on myself for all my mistakes and character flaws, but doing so is a distraction because I have the Lord on high with me, in me, moving my life on His trajectory. I need to keep my head up and my eyes focused toward heaven.

Apologize, pursue self-discipline, but don't get caught up

in the mess. It's a distraction at best and an idol at worst when we focus too much on getting ourselves together.

WHAT'S OUR PART?

So what is our part, and what is the part of the Holy Spirit?

If He molds us and ultimately does the work, and if we have this holy DNA from Jesus, what do we do?

Well, as for maturity, we can't speed it up—it happens over time. However, we can be open and available to the Holy Spirit, and we can participate in the maturing process by reading God's Word and keeping communion with God through meditation (contemplating the Word) and prayer.

So what about choice and self-discipline and managing our lives so we can enjoy them and make them better?

This is where work comes in.

Thank God I have the ability and freedom to make choices.

We can choose how we think and how we would like to live. We can't always change our circumstances, but we can choose our perspective. We can have a positive attitude and have faith and keep on in hope. And we can make physical changes to our lives. Does it come easy? Nope. But does a skilled pianist get to be excellent by just living? No! We become excellent by practicing and working hard, and we can become self-disciplined with some practice and hard work.

Get used to who you are.

There is so much freedom in stretching into yourself, being comfortable in who you are and how God made you. It's not only freeing, but it's really just lovely to settle into the you God made you to be.

Don't try to be somebody else; that's no fun at all! Plus it's one of the fastest ways to dislike your life! Accept who you are. If you don't know who you are, start figuring it out. Consider it an adventure! Have fun with it. Explore!

THE LONGING HEART AND DNA

God set the plans in motion for Paris to be a place to long for.

He put the artistry and pleasure and romance into the hearts of mankind, and that outpouring of what is inside us is what became Paris for me.

It's what becomes anything beautiful. God imprints Himself on us, weaving color into the essence of our souls, and we, in turn, let that beauty out to add glory to the world around us.

That's the thing, though, about what's inside of us. It's not all beauty. There is that marring, that blemish of sin that courses through us that also gets out and into the world. We can see the stain every day in our own relationships, on the news, and in our very thoughts.

We have great potential to bring pain and darkness into the world—or to bring glory and beauty and goodness.

My longing heart can be used for good or for bad. I can use my longings to be greedy and self-centered—to neglect my kids and my husband and do what I want—which will ultimately leave a trail of damage. Or I can use my longings to bring glory to my family, to the world, and to God. I can lay them at the feet of Jesus and walk them out by faith as I first love the people around me, caring for them and sacrificing for them.

We do get the choice.

But in both choices we don't kill off the longings. Our longings are in our God-given holy DNA, the DNA of His glory that He wants us to shine out to bring light to those in the world. Just like we can't change our eye color or hair color from the inside (we can only mask it), we can't change who God made us to be.

THE LONGINGS YOU HAVE AND THE COLOR OF YOUR SOUL

Just watch a child.

Yes, they have their sin natures we can see, but they also have a free-spiritedness that is a joy to watch. They also aren't afraid of their color—their innate beauty is often expressed in what interests them; their colors shine out and make the world a happier place. Kids aren't dull or gray; they are vivid little rainbows of life.

When God wove us together as human beings, I believe He used lots of color! God made the world around us vibrant, so why would He stop with us?

We are full of vibrancy that God planted into our very

souls, and it is that color that makes us want to be more than gray.

It's what makes us want to do more in life than just live. God's very glory and beauty is enwrapped in us so that we would reflect His glory in living bright and full lives for Him.

Joel N. Clark, author of *Awake*, is onto something when he says,

> When we fail to choose to live our lives fully awake, the ashes will extinguish the beauty, the mourning will smother the joy, and the despair will end our praise. When we sleep to the dreams inside our hearts, the message of love will become nothing more than a nice idea. Yet when we awaken to the dreams God has placed inside of us, our very lives become the beauty, magic, and wonder that the world needs.[20]

The color in us—our dreams and desires and longings—can be from God, and I would say that they are all from God; they just can get twisted or misplaced sometimes. We are all susceptible to that.

In his fantastic book *The Journey of Desire*, John Eldredge talks about how Christian, the protagonist from *Pilgrim's Progress*, mistakes the whispers from wicked ones as coming from his own mind. John says,

The crisis for Christian is that he did not know his own voice, his true voice. He was convinced that the whispers of the enemy were his own desires. Far too many Christians today make the same dangerous assumption—that every thought and desire they experience is their own.[21]

This is why we must be before the Lord, in faith, with our dreams and desires and longings, because then we will know God's voice. "My sheep hear My voice" (John 10:27), Jesus tells us.

Later in the book, Eldredge also challenges us to stay with the question Jesus asks in John 1:35-39 (NLT): "What do you want?" Stay with this question until you begin to get an answer.

So, let's come back to the simple question Jesus asks of us all: What do you want? Don't minimize it; don't try to make sure it sounds spiritual; don't worry about whether or not you can obtain it. Just stay with the question until you begin to get an answer.[22]

And here is my favorite part of the challenge Eldredge asks of us: "Once we know what we want, we must learn the grace of release."[23]

The grace of release.

Oh, how I love that phrase! How beautiful and kind and wise. The grace of release is being able to give our dreams back to God and trust Him with them. Because remember, He cares about us and He cares about our dreams. It doesn't mean all of our dreams will bloom the way we want them to, but it does mean He will make His love evident to us through them all.

DREAMS ARE IMPORTANT

When my children are left to their own devices, I can tell you that things in my house get crazy.

Not so much "things" but "children." The children get crazy.

Whenever I have a project I'm working on and our routine goes out the window for a few days, not only does my house look like a tornado went through it, but the kids get so whiney and unruly. They don't know what to do with themselves; they are desperate for direction. It reminds me of this wise saying:

> *Where there is no vision, the people are unrestrained.*
> PROVERBS 29:18

You have to admit that kids are such a great example of the whole human race; it's just that adults have (mostly) learned how to hide and/or control themselves. The Lord tells us that we need vision so that we can go forward with a sense of control, with a plan to stay on track. Just like children, if we don't have vision or a dream, we can feel out of control.

We need a dream to make a plan to go forward.

But here's the wild part: We need to release the plan to God and go forward in faith. Because the reality is, God might change the plan, divert the path, or take us a whole new way. Releasing our plans to Him is the definition of faith.

So we trust how God made us, what He put inside of us, and we go forward in faith. Now here's another part that is so important: the *why* of our longings.

The Lord gives us a dream in order to bring His Kingdom to bear on this earth in creative ways.

If the dream is from Him, and it aligns with how He wove us together, then we use that dream for His Kingdom.

WHAT HAPPENS WHEN YOUR DREAMS AND YOUR REALITY COLLIDE?

One of the areas I've struggled with is figuring out how to live in my reality while not trying to stuff away the color of my soul.

I want to feel alive and accept how God made me. I want to live out of who He made me to be. I also want to be content with the season I'm in—one that has little capacity to do all the things I dream up.

Because here's the thing: I'm not going to neglect my kids. And because of my small capacity, I can't go full steam ahead with my ideas and dreams. But I'm sure not going to kill my dreams, because that would be denying what God put in me. I am, however, learning how to temper my dreams in order to be wise with my time and kind and responsible with my family.

The fact is, my children—those beautiful eternal souls in my care—are my first priority; they are my people. They are the ones God gave me to disciple first and foremost. If I neglect them in order to minister to the many, I have lost my integrity. I must first minister to them, raising them in the fear of the Lord with love and grace and time and intention. They must come first. But I don't think that means I can't also minister to the many, as long as I'm living out the principle that Paul includes in his first letter to Timothy:

He must be one who manages his own household well,
keeping his children under control with all dignity
(but if a man does not know how to manage his own
household, how will he take care of the church of God?).

I TIMOTHY 3:4-5

Yes, this Scripture is out of context, as it's about an overseer or elder in the church. But I don't think I'm too far off by saying that this principle includes anyone who will be influencing and teaching others. They, too, should have their own homes in order. It has to do with integrity and faithfulness.

I don't expect to be a perfect mom, because that's absurd and ungodly to think I could ever get it completely right. I am a sinner-saint who is desperately dependent on God every day. And thank God He uses me in spite of myself. But I still believe there is wisdom in being faithful with our family first, because here's the thing: If my people are getting out of control, I need to stop whatever I'm doing and go after them.

In fact, that's exactly what I had to do with my sweet Caroline. I had to stop ministering to the many for a while (I quit the conference I was hosting) in order to go after her heart.

It was worth it.

I poured into her, and I got her back. Praise the Lord. But it is daily work, and I cannot take our relationship for granted. Mothering is my top priority, and I must commit to the integrity of putting my family first. Yep, I'm going to botch it a million and one ways, but I will get back up by His grace and through the power of the Holy Spirit and I will keep on.

And you can too.

Back to dreams for a moment.

My loftiest dream is to raise my children well, teaching them, nurturing them, and intentionally discipling them.

But I have other dreams—dreams of writing and speaking in order to encourage and inspire women to trust in and love the Lord their God with all their heart, mind, soul, and strength. I want to see women fully alive because their lives matter! I so dream of helping women to be set free and come to know the One who loves them and has purpose for them. My soul feels alive when I am able to write and speak to this end.

I know that God made me a visionary. I know He made me a wife and a mother, but He also gave me gifts to use in bringing His Kingdom to bear on this earth.

He also gave me a story. He set me free and put a new song in my mouth so that I would tell of His goodness in order that others would be set free.

The question remains, though: How do I do both and do both well?

For me, by understanding my capacity and my season, I choose to create times to purposely write and speak. I have a husband who is self-employed, and he is very supportive of the platform God has given to me to be able to reach women all over the world. In fact, whenever I want to quit, Jesse reminds me of all the letters I've received from women on how my words and story have impacted their lives for good. He prints out all the letters and puts them in a binder so we can one day look back at the legacy God has chosen to give to our family through what I've been able to do.

It's not about me or my merit. I am God's, and He will use me as He sees fit to do so. I will not push away His gift to me or deny what He has put inside me. Therefore, in obedience, I will steward the platform He gave me by faith, trusting Him to help me in all the details of life.

Also, again, there is the grace of release. I am aware that He can take this platform at any time.

He loves me and my husband and my kids, and as I'm before Him, in His Word, and attuned to His Spirit, I am able to make wise and discerning decisions about what I can and can't do. There is no formula; it is all by faith. I am fully aware that there are consequences to my choices, and so I am daily thinking through what is good and healthy and wise and what would be foolish or neglectful. I want to live by faith in the power of the Holy Spirit, following, obeying, and trusting God each day for the portion my family needs.

It is with these convictions that I am finally able to move forward as God leads. I am not *chasing* my dreams; I am simply accepting what God puts before me.

And I think that's the trick—not chasing dreams, but surrendering them and yourself to the Lord. You can map out a plan and still live by faith. To do this, you must be in His Word and must be vulnerable enough to let Him do what He needs to do in you before He can use you.

So yeah, there's laundry and dishes and homeschooling and writing, but there are also croissants to delight in, music to dance to, poetry that quickens the heart, adventures to generate memories, and so much more! God is so kind and artistic and creative; I just love how fun He is. I want to experience Him in all of it, without having to run away to do it.

I want to find His glory and magnificence in my everyday life. I want to let myself enjoy Him; I am accepting His love in all its forms.

I *can* choose to find the beauty and the joy and the adventure right where I am.

So who are you? What is your heart yearning for? How does that yearning bring light to your world?

Your DNA was not meant to be hidden. Just like the unique blue hue of your eyes or the red tint in your hair that all can see, your light is not meant to be hidden.

You are the light of the world—like a city on a hilltop that cannot be hidden. No one lights a lamp and then puts it under a basket. Instead, a lamp is placed on a stand, where it gives light to everyone in the house. In the same way, let your good deeds shine out for all to see, so that everyone will praise your heavenly Father.

MATTHEW 5:14-17, NLT

❧ Unearthing Your Longings

Who are you? What color did God put in your soul? Have you accepted and embraced who you are? Why or why not? What would it take for you to begin to believe that God made you wonderfully and for His purposes? Ask Him to show you who you are, and then . . . listen and wait and let Him reveal you.

Go deeper by meditating on Isaiah 64:8 and Psalm 139:13-16.

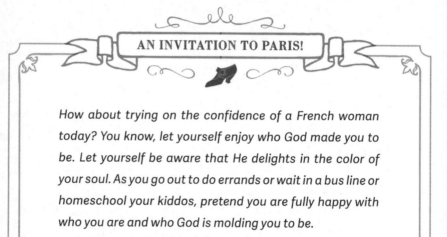

AN INVITATION TO PARIS!

How about trying on the confidence of a French woman today? You know, let yourself enjoy who God made you to be. Let yourself be aware that He delights in the color of your soul. As you go out to do errands or wait in a bus line or homeschool your kiddos, pretend you are fully happy with who you are and who God is molding you to be.

And just think, maybe one of these days, maybe even today, you will begin to live in the full confidence of who you are and who you are becoming.

8

CALLED TO SPARKLE

PARIS IS KNOWN as the City of Light, originally given that description because it was a vast center of education and ideas during the Age of Enlightenment (1650–1790), spurred by progressive thinkers and writers such as Voltaire. In 1828, Paris began lighting the Champs-Elysées with gas lamps, the first city in Europe to do so, earning it the nickname "La Ville-Lumière" or the City of Light.

Now where have I heard something like that before?

Ah, yes. "You are the light of the world. A city set on a hill cannot be hidden" (Matthew 5:14).

We are created and redeemed in order to be light. In some ways you could say we *are* Paris. But before we can be Paris, we need to be won over . . . wooed.

HOW GOD WOOED ME

My mom used to say that she thought I saw angels.

When I was a baby we would sit across from each other, and she told me I would look right past her and smile, as though I were looking at something wonderful. She was convinced it was angels.

When I was a young girl, during the summers when I would visit my mom, one of the things I would do with her is lie in bed with her at night and thank God for all sorts of things: puppy dogs and grass and sunshine and everything my young mind could come up with.

At home with my dad, where I lived most of the year, I kept a Bible next to my bed on the floor. I would pick it up from time to time and try to read it from the beginning like a book, but I could never get beyond page two.

I grew up going to a Catholic church with my stepmom, and although it was beautiful and I have lovely memories of dressing up for the Christmas service, I felt nothing in my soul spiritually while I was there.

But I always believed in God.

When I was probably around eight or nine, a traumatic event happened in my family, and I prayed and prayed that God would make things right. When the incident was finally resolved, I knew God had heard me, and it was then that He was forever cemented in heart.

In eighth grade I moved to Georgia to live with my mom. We didn't go to church, but my mom always told me she believed in Jesus. In my opinion, her actions and the way she lived didn't seem to reflect the little I knew about Jesus, but when she told me that she believed in Him, I felt she was being sincere.

I was so excited to finally live with my mom and my younger sister. At fourteen, I believed that a daughter should be with her mother, and finally I was. But it was soon apparent why my dad had kept me away; my mom relied on alcohol to get her through.

I know my mom loved me, and I believe she did her best with the wounded heart that she had, but it was an emotionally painful time for me.

But I wasn't alone. God continued to reveal Himself to me, gently leading me to Himself.

My uncle was visiting us, and since he knew I liked music, he gave me a Clay Crosse tape.

And here's the thing—I didn't even know there was such a thing as Christian music, let alone popular contemporary Christian artists. I thought the only songs that Christians sang were hymns. I don't know why on earth I actually listened to that tape, but I did.

As I was listening, I started crying. Through my tears, I prayed, "God, I don't know what any of this means, but I want whatever that man is singing about."

I didn't know that it was a person: Jesus.

I just knew my heart was broken and I needed help.

A little later, that same uncle took me to a church where people were singing and smiling and clapping—*What was this?* I had never seen anything like it before, but I thought immediately, *These are my people.*

My soul was stirred up, and I wanted to be a part of this kind of church, this kind of joy, this place where people seemed alive.

Oh, how He wooed me.

I didn't go to church consistently, and I still didn't really know who Jesus was or what Christianity was about, but my heart was wide open.

And then I got pregnant.

ALONE[24]

I was sixteen years old.

I was given a new name, and then I was drugged. I didn't like the IV. My dad held my hand, but I started to get really fidgety. They upped my drug dosage and wheeled me away. I was so cold, so they gave me a blanket. I counted backwards from 100 . . . 99 . . . 98 . . .

The end.

The end of my first baby's life.

It was always weird for me when I was pregnant with my firstborn, because people would always ask, "Is this your first?" I hated that question. I didn't know how to answer.

"Um, no, I killed my first baby. This will be my second." That wouldn't work. "My first is in heaven." That won't work either; people will think I miscarried. I landed on, "This is my husband's and my first."

It's been sixteen years since I had my abortion. Even though I have been forgiven and set free from the bondage I was once in, the memories of that time in my life and my fateful decision still hurt so deeply upon remembrance.

I'll never forget when I called to tell my dad I was pregnant. He was so kind and loving toward me. I'll also never forget the words out of my grandmother's mouth when I told her the same thing: "I'll take care of it." *What?* "No, I'm keeping the baby."

Three months later she had "it" taken care of.

The three months I was pregnant when I was sixteen were probably the three hardest months of my life. I was very sick, I felt very alone, and I was being torn in directions I wasn't prepared for. Everyone had a solution to my "problem," but no one wanted to hear mine. I wanted to keep the baby . . . at first. I figured I could get married and start a family.

After talking with others and hearing them tell me how I would miss such important things—like prom—if I had a baby I thought it would be better if I gave the baby to someone who couldn't have children. Nope, people didn't like that idea either.

During this time, my mom totally checked out of the situation. She almost became numb to the whole thing. She had her own demons to deal with and couldn't handle mine. My dad, a wonderful father, had decided that abortion probably was the better choice. I don't think he really believed that, but he had pressures of his own. One person in my life even wanted the baby for herself, but I couldn't bear that person raising my child.

Did I mention that my grandmother, who I thought was my best friend, stopped talking to me during this time? She wouldn't even look at me. The final straw was when my other grandmother came to visit me. She convinced me that having an abortion really would be the best decision. She spoke to me so kindly, and she showed me love. I was desperate for any sign that I was lovable at that point, so I agreed right then and there to have an abortion.

The night before the "procedure," I asked the baby to forgive me. I held my tummy and cried.

The day arrived, and my dad accompanied me to the hospital. Yes, the hospital, not the local abortion clinic. The doctor thought I would do better being at a hospital where I could be totally put under . . . drugged to unawareness.

I even had my name changed so that there would be no record that I had an abortion; I did have a fairly prominent family. That afternoon I didn't have an abortion; Sandy Charles did. Sandy Charles gave up hope that day; Sandy Charles let them stick a needle in her arm, drugs in her veins, and a murderer into her private domain. Sandy Charles offered her baby up for slaughter.

I slept for two days afterward. When I woke up, I was at my grandmother's, the one who wouldn't speak to me before but was now serving me toast with a smile. I had moved in with her—it was better that way. I ate the toast. Nothing was ever spoken about my abortion. It was a new day. It was like it never happened.

I lived with my mom for another year, and then I moved back in with my dad. At that point, I was a junior in high school, and I was ready to start over with a clean slate, a new life.

I made new friends, and no one knew about my past in Georgia.

I soon began attending Young Life, a Christian outreach to high school students. I went because that's what everyone did on Wednesday nights. But it was through Young Life that I began to finally start to understand who Jesus is.

And I wanted Him.

I began to listen more and pay attention and pray and try reading my Bible again. By my senior year, I knew I wanted to be a serious Christian; I wanted to follow God with all my heart.

I remember telling everyone around me about this Jesus. I just knew they would be so excited to hear about Him and that they, too, would want Him. I remember telling one friend in particular. She just listened and then said something like "That's nice."

That's nice! Don't you want Him too?

I couldn't understand why everyone didn't want to know this beautiful God-man who could—who *would*—redeem us and love us and make us new.

When I started at Penn State in 1999, I immediately got involved with The Navigators collegiate ministry, and

I began devouring the Scriptures. I would hide away in my dorm and read my Bible and write out all the verses that stood out to me. I couldn't get enough; it was alive to me. I understood the words. It was like scales had fallen off my eyes and I could see (see Acts 9:18).

I loved Jesus, but I was still a bit of a wreck. Oh, I followed Him and learned as much as I could, and I wanted Him so, but there was still this girl inside of me who felt very alone and very needy and who very much wanted to be loved. When those needs became overwhelming, I would do anything to numb them. I would go out and drink or find someone to spend the night with. I just couldn't be alone.

By my senior year of college, I was a disaster.

One night, tears poured down my face as I fell to my knees sobbing, crying out to the Lord, "What is wrong with me? I am at the bottom and can't go any lower. Please help me." Darkness crept all over my spirit, and I was worn down. My eyes were going dim, and my bones could barely hold up my flesh. I was in a pit of despair.

I waited patiently for the LORD; he turned to me and heard my cry . . .

I wanted to be a counselor, and I needed some experience for my résumé. I knew of a little place about two blocks from my apartment that might give me an internship. As I read over their application, one of the questions struck me: "What do you know about abortion?"

Nothing . . . Hmmm . . . I'd better get a book on it. Yes, I was that detached.

I found a book called *Forbidden Grief: The Unspoken Pain of Abortion* and set out to read it so I would be able to write an answer to the application question. I went to a little coffee shop and sat in a cushy chair with my notebook and pen all ready to take notes. That day, however, ink didn't fill the paper; tears did. I came face-to-face with my hidden pain.

He lifted me out of the slimy pit, out of the mud and mire . . .

I went back to the little place two blocks from my apartment. It happened to be a crisis pregnancy clinic. It also just happened to be a place that had a wonderful, kind, gentle, and loving woman who counseled women who've had abortions. I told her, "I think the Lord wants me to deal with my abortion."

She took me under her wing as we went through the Bible study *Forgiven and Set Free*.[25] She gave me a safe place to unabashedly experience all of my emotions—denial, anger, depression. (Yes, I was a perfect example of the stages of grief.) I was able to admit my sin, mourn my loss, and accept forgiveness and grace. I finally felt like my feet were beginning to be planted on something, *someone* real.

*He set my feet on a rock and gave me a firm place to
stand . . .*

I could finally hug women. Ha! I know that sounds
funny, but that is one of the ways I was healed. Part of my
pain included a mistrust of women, and if one tried to hug
me, even a friend, I got stiff. I was so walled up. Now, if you
ever meet me, please give me a great big hug and I will melt.
I am also able to watch prolife commercials and not leave the
room. I can smile when I see little children instead of tear
up. I can fully embrace my own children, knowing that it's
okay to enjoy them. God isn't going to punish me for my sin
of abortion—Jesus Christ already took that punishment for
me on the cross. I am free. You know what else? I can tell my
story. I am covered in grace and protection. . . . I am loved
and forgiven. The shame I once carried lies at the foot of the
cross; Satan has no power over me. God is the only one who
has the authority to tell me who I am . . . and I am His.

*He put a new song in my mouth, a hymn of praise to
our God. Many will see and fear the LORD and put
their trust in him.*

PSALM 40:1-3, NIV

Freedom is sweet and good, and I never want to go back.
Now I want to share with you one more thing God did
for me.

I really wanted to know the sex of my baby so I could

name him or her, and I asked the Lord to please tell me. The Lord gave me a dream. In my dream a blond-haired, bright-blue-eyed boy about seven or eight years old was hugging me and telling me it was okay. I kept telling him I was sorry, but he just kept saying it was okay and he'd see me again one day. His name was David.

> *He heals the brokenhearted and binds up their wounds.*
> PSALM 147:3, NIV

CALLED TO SHINE

Every time I go see my friend Karen, I cry. (She also makes my husband cry.)

There is something about entering into the vulnerable places of your heart with another person that just breaks and releases you. Karen is the woman I talk to when God brings issues up in my life that need to be dealt with. I sit on her couch, and I talk and we pray and we ask the Lord what it is I need to know or see or deal with.

Even though I go in willing, once I'm there I think I'm fine, until it's clear I'm not fine, and then I cry. I cry because the Lord reveals something in me that needs healing, and it hurts to uncover wounds, but it feels so good to acknowledge them so they can be healed. And it's because of this healing that I keep opening myself up to this process. You see, I've decided that I want a healthy relationship with myself.

I believe that the world is desperate for healthy people.

People who are willing to have the dark places turned into light.

And isn't it just lovely how God takes those dark places in our lives and offers to turn them into light?

We all have a story that is unfolding through our lives that won't be complete until heaven, but it all has purpose if we are willing to go through the dark to get to the light. We can choose to stay in our dark places—to be resentful and bitter and scared so that we don't grow and let light in—or not.

The Lord is tender and kind, and He will lead us toward freedom throughout our whole lives, and we have the opportunity to accept or reject His guidance. We can hide and act like we are okay, or we can get real vulnerable and walk through the fire in order to come out shining just a little bit brighter.

Let's say you are broken over something, and you cry out to God about it, and then the next day everything seems fine and you think, *Oh, it's really not a big deal.* Have you ever done that? That's the moment to make a move to deal with it and say, "Okay, God, I'm ready and willing." If you don't, I can assure you that "thing" will come up later—God always seems to bring things back until we deal with them.

When I first wrote my abortion story on my blog, I didn't want to do it.

It was painful and vulnerable, and I cried the whole time I was writing. But I believed with my whole heart that God wanted me to do it; it was like the last piece in my healing journey.

I hit publish and cried some more.

The reason I cried wasn't because I hadn't dealt with it; I cried because I was putting a very private thing out there for the whole world to see and judge. But you know what happened? Thousands of people viewed it, and so many women thanked me because it helped them know they weren't alone. And it helped them to seek healing and to understand that God is so loving and that there is always hope, that He wants us to come to Him for comfort.

He took a dark part of my story and gave it light so that others could see and hear and put their trust in the Lord.

Our stories aren't just for us—they are for those who are hurting and are in need of hope. We get to partner with God in being light-bearers for His Kingdom.

Whatever it is that you're in or have been in, if you stay tender and let God lead you through the healing, you will sparkle.

LIGHT

Light exposes, it guides, and it offers a new day.

When people are in the dark, everything is hidden, and when we hide, shame is there along with all the sin that we don't want others to see. Once we bring anything into the light, it is exposed—but it also sets us free because now it's out there for everyone to see. I know how scary it is to be found out. But when we are seen and our sin or our struggle is confessed, the enemy has no hold over us anymore because shame has been dismantled. Shame loves the dark; it loves when we hide because it can keep us in bondage. But in the light, it loses its strength over us.

I've seen this happen in the lives of others, and I've seen it in my own life. Whenever I hold things close because I'm afraid of what people will think, I stay locked up in shame and fear. But when I open myself up and let others into my dark places, and they love me anyway, I become free. We can open ourselves up and be rejected or made fun of or judged. We all know this happens. But when we find a safe place to share, we receive grace and love and are no longer locked up.

I remember when I was struggling with a dark sin, something in my mind, and I was scared to death to tell my husband or anyone else about it. But I was also desperate to be free.

So I took a risk.

I confessed my sin to Jesse.

When I finished, he said, "That's not so bad."

I was shocked. It was horrendous to me! Oh how the dark loves to magnify our struggles, making us feel dirty and so alone. How clever.

I decided to tell the women in my Bible study group. Again, I was scared, but I wanted prayer to be free. They barely blinked when I told them, and then they began to share their own dark places.

They helped me realize that I wasn't dirty or evil or weird or any of the lies the enemy uses to torment us and keep us silent. I was just a human being living with a human mind that is bent toward sin, as we all are. But it took safe people to help me see the truth.

I want to be a safe person because I know how much I need safe people.

As the saying goes, *Treat other people the way you want to be treated.*

Exposure makes what's hidden lose its power. Take the example of a child who is afraid of the dark. When you hear your child crying, you run to the child's bedroom and turn on the light. Suddenly, the darkness vanishes and with it, the power to frighten your child. Light changes everything.

The other thing that I love about the light is that it gives us the opportunity to start over. God's mercies are new every morning (see Lamentations 3:22-23). A new day means we can forget what happened the night before and begin again. And it is in the light that we can see clearly to know where to go.

We can also be a light to others to help them break free of shame, to know the hope of a new day, and to see where to go. We can lead them with our stories and with the light that God has given us. Once we've been healed of something (and there are plenty of "somethings" throughout our lifetime), we become leaders of light. We shine so that others can see there's a way forward, hoping they will ultimately see Him. All light leads to the Light Giver, because He is the one who saves and heals and frees. He is light.

LOOK AROUND YOU FOR WHERE YOU CAN SHINE

Sometimes I wonder if good works have been relegated to physically meeting needs outside our homes. There seems to be an unspoken consensus that if our good works are only done in the home—at least for a time—that we aren't doing enough. That we need to do something bigger for God.

What if my good works are being faithful to my family—loving and supporting my husband, teaching my children about God and the world they live in, taking care of my home and being hospitable? What if the daily things such as feeding my children, bathing them, showing them how to properly brush their teeth, helping them learn to read and how to speak kindly to a friend who has hurt them—what if those are my good works? Is that enough for God?

As I crawl out of this season and into a new one, what if the expansion of my good works is keeping an eye out in my neighborhood for needs I can meet?

What if I never serve in a soup kitchen or go on a mission trip to another country? Will God still be pleased with me?

Are my daily meager offerings enough?

Maybe I'm not as selfish as I think. I mean, maybe being faithful where I am is enough, and I shouldn't feel guilty.

I think the guilt comes when we know we should do something and we don't do it. When we spend time in God's Word and with the Spirit, we will be more receptive to what He calls us to do day in and day out, in the various seasons of our lives, because where we are now is not necessarily where we will be in the future. It's why we follow the Spirit; we don't know where it comes from or where it is going, but we follow by faith.

I think the same is true for good works. We follow by faith as God leads us to what He wants us to do. If we are open, it means that we are open to whatever He asks of us, whether it is to care for orphans in a third-world country (Are we open to that?), to faithfully raise our children with diligence and intention (Are we open to that?), to adopt a child (Are we open to that?), or a great many other things God may have planned for us. The question is, are we open and willing?

The only thing we're not allowed to do is nothing.

God commands us to love and serve and do something. That "something" looks different for everyone, but Jesus is clear: Go.

Go raise your kids well.
Go feed the hungry.
Go visit prisoners.
Go clothe the poor.
Go love your neighbor practically.
Go share your hope.
Go care for a widow.
Go help an orphan.
Go make disciples.
Go carry your cross.

SEPTEMBER'S STORY[26]

My friend September McCarthy responded to God's command to love and serve and do something. I want to share her story with you.

> While raising a family has become my purpose, my vision is to change the world. One life at a time. My husband and I are working to teach our children to be difference breakers and not distance makers. There is a divine plan of influence that has handed us the light of Jesus and asked us to hold it high.
>
> Although it would be easier to tuck our light safely in at night and work through a simple and safe routine every day at home, we have been working to stretch ourselves out into our own community for years and allowing Christ to make those divine appointments. It seemed like a simple thing—to bake loaves of bread and deliver them throughout our community. This is what happened:
>
> I packed up the children into our fifteen-passenger van, with wrapped loaves of bread and some handwritten notes from our family. Our plan was to drive around until we saw someone who we thought might need some warm bread or deliver it to someone who we knew needed encouragement. Baking more bread than our twelve family members can eat and taking a morning once a week to shine

God's light hasn't always been easy; there have been complaints at times. But we believe it is a training ground for all of us so that we can see—and listen to—His Spirit, His power, and His presence. Simply put, we had willing hearts and we wanted to be used.

We made our deliveries until there were only two loaves left. I waited to see if our children had any suggestions on where to go. And then I thought of a home that sits across the road from our church. Every Sunday morning, I would notice a man about my age who would sit in his lawn chair and watch us come and go. He'd also see us come and go to weeknight services or volunteer as a family on church workdays. We'd wave, and he'd wave back. But we did not know him. We had invited his family to special occasions and services at church, but I never got his name.

I could see that the children were growing restless in the back of the van. *I know You must have someone special waiting for this bread, God.* We were directly in front of the church. I glanced across the street, but the man wasn't in his lawn chair. *Stop. Stop here now.* If the nudge were any stronger, it would have been audible.

I pulled into the driveway of the home and shifted the van into park. Suddenly I was bombarded by a lot of questions and chatter from the children.

"Is this who we are giving the bread to, Mommy?"
"Here? Really, here?"

The house seemed extremely still and empty. I
sent one of the children to the front door with the
bread. No one answered the knocks on the door.
That's strange. I thought for sure this was where we were
supposed to stop today. After I rebuckled every one
of the kids' seat belts, I shifted the van into reverse,
then paused. "Why are you waiting, Mom?"

Just then the front door opened and the man
came out, walking slowly toward the van. He looked
different to me—sullen and discouraged. As he got
closer, the children were all talking a mile a minute,
excited that our bread would find a home. I rolled
my window down, while waving my right hand
behind me to hush the children's questions and
excitement. I smiled. He waited.

I broke the awkward silence. "We were in town
and brought you some bread. We don't know if you
can use it, but we wanted to say hello and leave
you a little note of encouragement." More silence.
I was worried now. *Holy Spirit, lead me.* And then
the very stoic man began to cry. Tears were rolling
down his cheeks, and he was standing at my window
unabashedly indicating that he was broken. *I AM,*
I need You.

He spoke in slow, grieving tones. His daughter
had just given birth to premature twins. They didn't

survive, and the entire family was numb, in a state of shock. He mumbled that he was working on funeral details. He gasped for some air and almost choked. I reached my hand through the van window and rested it on his shoulder.

Fourteen years earlier, I had lost identical twin boys in my womb. I have been to the grave. I have buried my babies. God gave me the words to share with this wounded grandfather. "I am so, so sorry for your loss. So very sorry." We shared tears, and for the first time in over an hour everyone in the van was hushed.

I almost forgot to hand him the bread, an afterthought to why God really wanted us there that day. This wasn't about breaking bread. This was about the Hope that is within me. The One who fed the multitudes.

No one said a word as I backed our van out of the man's driveway. Seeing is more than believing. It is knowing. Divine appointments are everywhere.

What is your story? What have you gone through or are going through that can bring hope and light to someone else?

Or maybe right now you need to see the light of someone else and just rest for a while until you feel safe enough to enter healing. It's not easy to be exposed, and it's not easy to go through a healing process. It's usually extremely painful, and it takes time. There is no easy fix to a hurting soul. And the reality is, there is always more than one thing that needs attention, because we are complex people with a variety of issues and wounds and history. But God gives reprieve; He doesn't give us everything at once, even if sometimes it feels like He does. His goal is always to show you how much He loves you and have you trust Him with your whole life, no matter what happens. He wants your soul to delight in being completely abandoned to Him alone.

And when we are His alone, Paris has nothing on us, because we were created and redeemed to sparkle brighter than any city ever could.

Shine on, sister. You were made for this.

✑ Unearthing Your Longings

What is your story? What has God done in your life? Think of how He has brought light to your broken places, your wounds, your darkness. How can you let the light of your story shine to those around you? Be free to sparkle because you were made to shine.

Go deeper by meditating on Psalm 40:1-3 and Isaiah 61:1-3.

AN INVITATION TO PARIS!

There's no argument that Paris illuminated at night is enchanting, but not nearly as enchanting as a dark night filled with the glow of stars. Just like the stars break up the dark with light, you break up the dark because you are light. Put down a blanket in your backyard and lie down with someone dear to you, and look up at the very metaphor that is you. Or go to a planetarium and sit in awe of the beautiful wonder of the universe that God spoke into being.

And remember, the same stars you are seeing are the same stars someone in Paris is seeing as well. We are all under the glow, and we all have the opportunity to shine.

9
HOME

It wasn't Paris, but it was beautiful.

All over social media were pictures from people I knew who were spending time in Tuscany, Italy, and I just about died with envy.

There were pictures of wine and foods that were all colors of the rainbow. Petite coffee mugs with steaming coffee, tarts filled with berries, magnificently bright red flowers, enchanting stone buildings, and breathtaking views of the green landscape and watercolor-blue skies filled up my screen, and my heart nearly pounded out of my chest. Tears glazed over my eyes because I longed to be there so much that I ached.

I wanted Tuscany. I wanted beauty and wide-open spaces and to smell the aroma of warm bread next to fresh cut flowers under a canvas sky newly painted with rainbows.

I was made for Tuscany. I was made for Paris. I was made for all the beauty in the world because . . .

I was made for heaven.

Home is that place where you feel loved and known and secure and fully yourself: You always want to go back there.

Even if you were in Paris, you would, at some point, want to go home.

Home, where my family and friends and roots are. Whenever I'm on a trip or a vacation, no matter how wonderful it is, I am always glad to be going home at the end of it. Because at home I can really rest; I can settle in.

Jesus says we can come to Him and He will give us rest (see Matthew 11:28-30). Jesus is the rest we can enter into. And He is the Kingdom come. There is a place of Kingdom come, a place of rest where He is.

It's like the Word.

Jesus is the Word made flesh, and yet we have His Word to read that is alive and sharp (see Hebrews 4:12). He is the Word, and He speaks to us through the Word.

We enter His rest, and we will one day enter His place of rest.

This home, where we can finally and fully settle in, is the place where all our longings begin and all our longings end. It is the Kingdom come; it is our heavenly home.

I am longing for Paris because it's beautiful, and it inspires something in me.

I am longing for heaven because it's my home.

And my home is the place where all the beauty began and where it will fill me up and meet my deepest needs, because I will be with the beautiful One.

For I consider that the sufferings of this present time are not worthy to be compared with the glory that is to be revealed to us. For the anxious longing of the creation waits eagerly for the revealing of the sons of God. For the creation was subjected to futility, not willingly, but because of Him who subjected it, in hope that the creation itself also will be set free from its slavery to corruption into the freedom of the glory of the children of God. For we know that the whole creation groans and suffers the pains of childbirth together until now. And not only this, but also we ourselves, having the first fruits of the Spirit, even we ourselves groan within ourselves, waiting eagerly for our adoption as sons, the redemption of our body.

ROMANS 8:18-23

All my longings—this pull that seems to rise up from my soul and make me lean a little more in and a little more up—they are the stir of heaven, the magnet attracting me to itself.

I am drawn toward my home. No matter where I'm grounded here on this earth, no other attraction will meet with the force of my heart and heaven. It cannot, because my heart and my soul and all of me was made for God and His Kingdom. All my longings, all the stirrings, they are there so I know that I have a home waiting for me and that nothing on this earth will fully meet my needs. Only glimpses, only pieces of the beauty here will give me a taste. The banquet is for when I go home.

HOME IS WHERE WE ARE KNOWN

Mark Buchanan has this wonderful quote: "Life doesn't justify living. Only eternity does."[27]

Everything can go wrong in life, but eternity justifies living. It justifies how we live or what we do or how we think. I feel like eternity has to shape our dailiness. Eternity has to shape our perspective. There are days when the only thing that keeps me going, keeps my head above water, is eternity. I'm trying to have that eternal perspective, recognizing the fact that it isn't some far-off thing.

At this moment, we are walking in the "Kingdom come." Jesus made that clear when He answered the Pharisees in Luke 17:20-21:

> One day the Pharisees asked Jesus, "When will the Kingdom of God come?"
>
> Jesus replied, "The Kingdom of God can't be detected by visible signs. You won't be able to say, 'Here it is!' or 'It's over there!' For the Kingdom of God is already among you." (NLT)

When we know Jesus, the Kingdom to come—the Kingdom we long for—is set in our hearts.

In the Gospel of John, Jesus prays a beautiful prayer to His Father about His disciples—but also about us:

They do not belong to this world any more than I do. Make them holy by your truth; teach them your word, which is truth. Just as you sent me into the world, I am sending them into the world. And I give myself as a holy sacrifice for them so they can be made holy by your truth.

I am praying not only for these disciples but also for all who will ever believe in me through their message. I pray that they will all be one, just as you and I are one—as you are in me, Father, and I am in you. And may they be in us so that the world will believe you sent me.

I have given them the glory you gave me, so they may be one as we are one. I am in them and you are in me. May they experience such perfect unity that the world will know that you sent me and that you love them as much as you love me. Father, I want these whom you have given me to be with me where I am. Then they can see all the glory you gave me because you loved me even before the world began!

JOHN 17:16-24, NLT

The walk to heaven is already underway for those of us who believe in the gospel and Jesus Christ. Hebrews 10:14 says,

> *For by that one offering he forever made perfect those who are being made holy.* (NLT)

What offering? Jesus' life offered on the cross for our sins. We are the ones who are in the process of being made holy, but we're already perfect according to heaven. Well, how can we be complete and yet incomplete at the same time? It's this amazing paradox we don't get. While we are working out our salvation here on earth, we are at the same time, according to heaven, already perfect and complete because of Jesus. When we finally enter heaven, it will be like a kiss. All of a sudden our perfection will actually be realized, even though it's already realized according to heaven.

And not only is our perfection complete, but who we are is fully realized in heaven.

One day I'm going to be me fully realized.

I always tell my children that before they were born they were in the mind of God. And that's something, isn't it? That He had us, all of us, in His mind before we ever came to be. He destined us, He formed us, and He allowed an ache to be birthmarked into us so that we may never be fully satisfied on this earth. We would always be missing something, wanting something, yearning for something more. We would tilt our souls toward whatever gave us pleasure and a sense of filling, but whatever that thing was, it would never fully satisfy our hunger for more.

THE ACHE FOR SOMETHING MORE

"If we find ourselves with a desire that nothing in this world can satisfy, the most probable explanation is that we were made for another world."
C. S. LEWIS

I have never ached for heaven the way I have after reading the book *Peace Like a River*, a story told through an eleven-year-old boy's eyes as he and his family go on a search for his outlaw brother.

This novel by Leif Enger has the most compelling, beautiful, soul-tugging *description* of heaven I have ever encountered. In fact, it's so good that I'm hesitant to share even a bit of it with you because it will be out of context, but I'll share a few lines:

> Near the shore the water appeared gold as on your favorite river at sunup, but farther out it turned to sky and cobalt and finally a kind of night in which the opposite shore lay hidden.
>
> At that moment I had no notion of identity. Nor of burden. I laughed in the place of language. . . . The meadow was layered with flight. In fact it seemed there was nothing that couldn't take wing. Seized with conviction I spread my arms and ran for

it. Nope, no liftoff—but I came close! At times my feet were only brushing the ground. . . . The place had a master! Realizing this, I knew he was already aware of me—comforting and fearful knowledge. Still I wanted to see him. The farther I went the more I seemed to know or remember about him.[28]

You really must get a hold of this book ASAP. The whole heaven scene, the way Leif describes it, makes something in me rise, confirming I am meant for a place of freedom and beauty and filling.

The closest I ever *felt* to what it would be like in heaven was in a dream I had.

In that dream . . .

I ran. (Which is interesting because I hate running. Not my thing.)

Really, it was more like gliding. And there was no pain in it, just freedom. I felt wonderful. As I ran and glided effortlessly down a long road, this verse came to me:

> *But they who wait for the LORD shall renew their strength; they shall mount up with wings like eagles; they shall run and not be weary; they shall walk and not faint.*
>
> ISAIAH 40:31, ESV

I ran, and I thought about heaven, and I thought about the wind on my face.

No tired legs.

No twisted ankles.

No gasping for breath.

No side aches.

I just ran.

My new body fit the inside me perfectly.

My spirit was not held back.

It was glorious.

Glorious.

I felt absolutely light and free, and I knew I would one day experience what was in my dream.

My longings are the reminder that there is more—another world, another place where I am meant to be.

HOW DO I LIVE HERE IN THE MEANTIME?

When Jesse and I were first married, we lived in a small one-bedroom apartment I was already renting. Situated between two Penn State frat houses in downtown State College, we were used to the loud nights and college ruckus from the students. We loved our little apartment and spent many nights having friends over and entertaining. It was fun and sweet and just right for newlyweds.

Then one day I went to a friend's house. Keyword *house*. Right then and there I was bitten by the envy bug. Our cute little apartment didn't seem so cute anymore; instead, I began thinking of it as a pit stop to something better. I wanted a house.

We couldn't afford a house. Jesse was a full-time college student working at a hot dog joint, while I was working at a crisis pregnancy clinic, where my salary was generated by fundraising. There would be no house in our immediate future.

Nonetheless, I spent hours house-hunting online, dreaming of rooms to decorate, space to entertain, and raising a family in a "real" home.

Before long, I was pregnant. It was a happy surprise. The ache for a "real" home still lingered, but I had no choice but to get our apartment ready for a baby, so I did. We didn't have room for a crib, so we got a Pack 'n Play and put it right next to our bed. There was barely walking room between it and our bed. I emptied out a closet and made room for clothes and burp cloths and all the wonderful trappings that go with having a baby on the way. The changing table went at the foot of our bed, and under it went the diapers and wipes and washcloths. Such fun preparing for a baby! When our precious little girl arrived, we settled her right into her new nursery—our bedroom. It worked out great for late night feedings as she was right next to me to grab.

By the time she was three months old, my husband had received a job offer from another town two hours away. It was only twenty minutes from his hometown, where his parents still lived, so we packed up and moved in with them temporarily while we searched for a house.

A house! Finally!

It all seemed providential because after two months, we found a wonderful little home, a duplex with a large front porch and hardwood floors. It was small, but lovely. Just right for our small family. We were grateful that the time had come where we could get our very own *home*.

Another baby came, and then another, and I was bitten once again.

I was ready for a better home, something bigger, with a yard and closet space. However, it seemed clear that we were not going to be moving, and so I decided on the best—and really only—solution for a heart to be happy: contentment. I prepared my mind that this would be our forever home, and so I treated it as such. I cared for it, decorated it, and planned to spend many years building memories in that little duplex.

And then one day while Jesse and I were in the car, he said, "It's time to look for a new home, one in the town I'm working in." Both our hearts were suddenly prepared for a move (which we took as a sign from the Holy Spirit that He would be moving us), and we kept our eye out for a house. As it turned out, neighbors of Jesse's parents were planning on moving. It was another duplex, but a bit bigger and more updated, with a yard and closet space! We asked the sellers if they would hold off putting it on the market and sell it to us when our house sold. They agreed. Right before we were going to put our house on the market, we met someone looking for a house. Within three days our house was sold to that family, and we were able to get the new house next to Jesse's parents. Seamless.

I am writing these words in my sweet little home. We've

been here for five years now, and I feel settled. But I have days where I feel the sting of the initial bite of wanting something more. I know about contentment, and the wisdom of being content, but the truth is, my heart still longs for something more. This time, I envision a small farm with wide spaces for my children to run around in and explore. I don't know if I'll ever have that little farm, and I'm quite thankful and content to have a home at all, but somewhere inside is a small voice that says, "Don't settle in completely because you might have to pack everything up and move."

And so I hesitate to be fully *home*. Do I really want to put in the work and money to make this house our home? Do I really want to invest?

I want to enjoy this life, enjoy my God, live out His purposes, and be content where He has me, for however long. The important thing isn't settling in or not; it's how tightly I'm holding on to where I'm settling. I keep my hands open and loose, ready to toss things in boxes if need be.

Yes, I'm making this earth my home, for the time being. But when it's time to go to where I really belong, to where I come from, where I was thought up and destined from, I'll be overjoyed.

What I really want, what I'm really longing for is a place to settle into that is my forever home, a place where I can really rest.

There is a rest when you know you are home for good and you don't have to worry about packing up and leaving. It's just, *home*. And it feels good to cozy into something that is yours.

Heaven is ours, friends. It is ours, sisters and brothers, children of the One who is preparing a place for us to settle into, a forever home.

Paris will leave me thirsting for more, and it will ultimately let me down, because I wasn't made for Paris. I was made for all the things that I long for in Paris: beauty, art, culture, romance, light, and joy.

THE PAIN OF UNFULFILLED EARTHLY LONGING

Take a walk with me through the desert as we observe the man who stood in the cleft of the rock and saw the glory of God.

Moses was chosen to lead the Israelites to freedom and to a new land that boasted of goodness and delight, a place to call home. It was this Promised Land that the Israelites put their hope in. They would finally have a place of their own after so much hardship and wandering.

And finally, after forty years, it was time. They would prepare to go into the land. But Moses would not be able to go.

Moses, the man who talked with God, who spent time in the presence of God, and whose face shone because he was so close to God, was not allowed to go. Why? Why did this faithful servant and friend of God not get to go into the Promised Land?

Because it turns out, according to God, he lacked faith.

During a time in the desert when the people couldn't get water, they began to complain and get angry with Moses and Aaron (Moses' brother). This was the second time the people grumbled about not having water. The first time, near the beginning of their wilderness journey, God told Moses to strike a rock and water would come forth. Moses did as the Lord commanded. Now it seemed they were in the same situation. So Aaron and Moses went to the Lord for help. The Lord spoke to Moses:

> *Take the rod; and you and your brother Aaron assemble the congregation and speak to the rock before their eyes, that it may yield its water. You shall thus bring forth water for them out of the rock and let the congregation and their beasts drink.*
>
> NUMBERS 20:8

Did you notice the difference? This time, the Lord did not tell Moses to strike the rock with a rod; He said to speak to it. But Moses said to them,

> *"Listen now, you rebels; shall we bring forth water for you out of this rock?" Then Moses lifted up his hand and struck the rock twice with his rod; and water came forth abundantly, and the congregation and their beasts drank. But the LORD said to Moses and Aaron, "Because you have not believed Me, to treat Me as holy in the sight of the sons of Israel, therefore you shall not bring this assembly into the land which I have given them."*
>
> NUMBERS 20:10-12

God saw Moses, and He saw that Moses did not believe Him. Moses relied on the rod instead of the words he was to speak. Which is interesting, because the whole reason Aaron was with Moses was because Moses was afraid to speak; he didn't feel qualified. But Moses had pleaded with the Lord,

> *O Lord, I'm not very good with words. I never have been, and I'm not now, even though you have spoken to me. I get tongue-tied, and my words get tangled.*
>
> EXODUS 4:10, NLT

After all the years spent with God, Moses still didn't believe Him.

I think the tragedy is that Moses didn't believe that he was enough, even though God had called him. Moses used a prop, instead of the words God had given him, to be used to bring relief to the people.

It was because of this that Moses did not enter the Promised Land. The Lord allowed him to see it, but not enter it.

> *Then the LORD said to him, "This is the land which I swore to Abraham, Isaac, and Jacob, saying, 'I will give it to your descendants'; I have let you see it with your eyes, but you shall not go over there." So Moses the servant of the LORD died there in the land of Moab, according to the word of the LORD.*
>
> DEUTERONOMY 34:4-5

And there it is, our earthly understanding. We read the story of Moses and we see that he did not enter the Promised Land.

Now let's back up a minute and see the story from a heavenly perspective, something we are not usually privy to until heaven. But here it is: Moses did not enter the earthly Promised Land, but where did he go when he died that day on the mountain? He went to the ultimate Promised Land, the heavenly one. He stepped directly into what he longed for nearly his whole life—he just didn't know it until he got there.

Friends, this is the thing about our longings, the deep, ultimate longings of our souls: They will all be fulfilled in a moment when we step into the heavenly Promised Land.

Some of our longings only dip into the soul, say like traveling the world. But other longings are groans of heartache that we feel just might kill us on this earth. The mom who is groaning because she lost her baby to cancer. The girl who is enslaved in a brothel and groaning to be free. There is pain and grief that is beyond what we can handle, but the truth is, while the pain of this earth can be crushing, there is coming a day when the joy will crush the pain. The girl who believes will be free, and the mom who sets her heart on Jesus will see her baby.

When I had that dream about my boy David and how he smiled and hugged me and told me he'd see me again one day, I believed it. I believe God gave me that dream to comfort me and to remind me that there is a heavenly perspective that will rock my world one day. I will get it. I will understand, somehow, that God is so much more loving than I can even comprehend on this sin-shattered earth.

IT'S ALL TO MAKE US LONG FOR HOME

All of it, all the music and art and color and wonder and taste and smell and magnificence, it's all for us, for our souls, to delight in and long after. In the middle of all the darkness and sin, there are these places of light that call our souls home. Paris can only ever give me a glimpse of the true thing I yearn for: to be with my God in all of His splendor.

And to be with Him is to be home, which must be very good.[29]

Yes, it will be very good to be with our Father, and He has a place for us that is more beautiful than Paris or Tuscany or whatever exquisite place that holds your imagination.

The heavens and the earth will pass away, and there will be a new heaven and a new earth (see Isaiah 65:17), and we will be made for it, for that place with no pain or tears or death or unfulfilled longings. I believe that in that moment when our souls are lifted into eternity, all our longings will be met.

There is a current heaven that Jesus calls a place of "Paradise" (Luke 23:43). Paul also uses the word *Paradise* for it (2 Corinthians 12:4). It's a place where Jesus is seated right now at the right hand of the Father. Can we understand this? Can we wrap our minds around it? Of course not. The things of heaven are beyond our wildest imaginations. Why do you think there are atheists? They lack imagination;

they cannot accept that God doesn't work inside our limited understanding. What we know, what we can comprehend, is that there is a place we will be forever, and it will be good and beautiful.

He will wipe away every tear from their eyes; and there
will no longer be any death; there will no longer
be any mourning, or crying, or pain; the first things
have passed away.

REVELATION 21:4

It is home where all of our longings will be fulfilled.

My longing for Paris will be fulfilled because my deep longing for beauty and love and community will be fulfilled.

The source of that longing was put there so that you and I would never be fulfilled here. Nothing will fulfill us long-term on this earth. We will get close, at times, and we will have moments of filling, but those moments will pass. Just as the longing reminds us that we are not yet home, the glimpses of home will remind us just how good it will be.

If I go to Paris and my husband kisses me under the stars next to the Eiffel Tower, I will get a glimpse. If while in Paris I eat the most delectable, delicious food, I will get a glimpse. If I see a couple dancing on the street or a musician singing to the tune of his gift, I will get a glimpse. If I go into the Louvre and see the finest art, I will get a glimpse. And if I go into the Paris countryside and lie down in a field of flowers under the wild blue, I will yet again, get a glimpse.

All this beauty and goodness was inspired by God, and the reason it makes our hearts quicken is because it was meant to.

That first kiss with your love? It was meant to make you fly.

Again, it is these things that draw us to the God who is artist, lover, musician, and dancer.

And one day, we will be with Him. We will be home. And all our longings will be fulfilled.

✑ Unearthing Your Longings

You were made to have longing in your soul because you were made for another world. When you long for something, you have the opportunity to remember heaven, the place you belong and where you are known. What are you longing for? How does that longing, the root of it, remind you of heaven?

Go deeper by meditating on Romans 8:18-23 and Revelation 21:4-8.

AN INVITATION TO PARIS!

Go into your town or the nearest city and get lost, as if you were in Paris. Wander around, guided solely by whim. See something beautiful you want to ponder? Look and reflect. See a lovely little café you want to pop into? Sit awhile and indulge. Enjoy your discoveries, and when you're ready, go home. Draw yourself a warm bath or tuck yourself in your favorite chair and thank God that one day you will be settled in your forever home.

AFTERWORD

SARAH WAS IN a funk; I don't know how else to describe it. I could see the tension building up within her, unsettling her, and I could sense she was longing for something more.

Occasionally it would play out in our conversations—she wanted to go to Paris, to travel, and to meet and connect with women from across the world. But she knew how important her family was to her and how she was needed here. When I saw Sarah choose to be intentional about taking charge of her longings and come to a decision in her heart that there were some desires that would go unresolved for a period of time, possibly forever, I saw Sarah no longer dwelling in a place of stagnancy, but growth. Seeing her choose the things she had control over and pursuing them expanded her mindset in ways she hadn't foreseen. She wanted to live fully right where she was. Suddenly a spark came alive in her that I haven't seen in a long time. Because of it, she's grown as a mother, and the relationships she has with our children have become all the better. Even our marriage has been strengthened. The mental shift in perspective led to a physical shift in our family dynamic.

Her journey was inspiring to me, as it helped me take ownership of my own life and my own tensions that I have been wrestling with. I truly believe that when you choose, as Sarah says, "to live wide awake" that you will not only encounter positive change in your own life, but the health of your family will prosper as well. I hope and pray that each one of you will experience a life lived fully in the midst of where you are.

Jesse

33 SEARCH-YOUR-HEART QUESTIONS

Search me, God, and know my heart; test me and know my anxious thoughts. See if there is any offensive way in me, and lead me in the way everlasting.

PSALM 139:23-24, NIV

OPEN YOURSELF UP to the leading of the Holy Spirit by praying the above Scripture before you begin. Ponder the following questions and consider talking them over with a trusted friend or group of friends. Have your Bible near for any Scriptures that the Lord brings to mind, and feel free to stop and pray through whatever the Lord leads you to. You may need to take time, days even, between questions. Remember, it is not your destiny to be unfulfilled, but to walk in confidence as a delighted-in daughter of God.

1. Are there any areas of your life that you don't feel you can trust God with fully?

2. What fears stand in the way of putting your complete trust in Him?

3. What disappointments have you experienced that have caused you to hold back from trusting Him?

4. What is your greatest fear in handing over every area of your life to Him?

5. If your greatest fear comes true, is it settled in your heart that God is still good?

6. Are you angry with God about anything?

7. If so, what's causing that anger?

8. How do you believe God views you?

9. How do you view God?

10. Do you see Him as happy or as angry?

11. Where does your perception of God come from?

12. Is there something in your life you haven't dealt with yet because you feel it would be too painful?

13. Can you trust God with that thing?

14. Do you have a dream or a longing in your soul?

15. How do you believe God views your dreams and longings?

16. What is the motivation behind your dream?

17. Is God ultimately glorified if your dream comes to fruition?

18. What gifts has God put inside you to bring His Kingdom to bear on this earth in creative ways?

19. What season are you in, and what are you realistically capable of at the moment?

20. Are you using your gifts—whether in your home, your neighborhood, your church, or in the world— to a realistic capacity, or are you in a season of raising little ones, where you need to just mother and rest when you get the chance?

21. Who are you listening to on a daily basis?

22. Where are you being fed spiritually?

23. Are the people who influence you encouraging you in grace and maturity?

24. Do you need to make any changes to the things you see, read, or listen to?

25. Do you know that you are loved?

26. Do you know that you are chosen—that you were in the heart and mind of God before you were even knit together?

27. Do you know Jesus personally?

28. Have you felt the warm embrace of His love?

29. Do you know that if you are His child you are a delight to Him?

30. Do you know that He wants you to experience joy and pleasure, that He made it for you?

31. Are there any other areas of your life that you need God to unfold for you so you can have understanding and heal?

32. Are you ready for healing?

33. What steps can you take to begin the healing process?

For further reflection, meditate on the following Scriptures:

He has redeemed my soul from going to the pit,
And my life shall see the light.

JOB 33:28

Far be it from God to do wickedness,
And from the Almighty to do wrong.

JOB 34:10

The LORD is near to the brokenhearted
And saves those who are crushed in spirit.

PSALM 34:18

Give thanks to the LORD, for He is good,
For His lovingkindness is everlasting.

PSALM 136:1

Taste and see that the LORD is good;
How blessed is the man who takes refuge in Him!

PSALM 34:8

The LORD your God is in your midst,
A victorious warrior.
He will exult over you with joy,
He will be quiet in His love,
He will rejoice over you with shouts of joy.

ZEPHANIAH 3:17

ACKNOWLEDGMENTS

I ACKNOWLEDGE FIRST and foremost the work of the Holy Spirit over my life, the kindness of God, and the grace given to me through Jesus Christ.

Jesse, you have championed me from the start, and I cannot begin to thank you for how you have lifted me up. You have loved me, supported me, spoken truth to me when I believed lies, and been my hero. You are my best friend. I love you.

Ella, Caedmon, and Caroline, you are my most favorite people, and I am so glad I get to do life with you. Thank you for your patience and grace as I worked on this book. I love you so.

Mom, I see you and I see light. You are a miracle, and you are brave, and I see the art in your soul. Even though we've had some killer hard times, we've made it. We haven't given up on each other. You were the first person to introduce me to God with your nightly prayers and your stories of how God intervened in your life. You put a smile in my heart when you told me I used to see angels. And it was you who passed on to me the gift and desire to write. Thank you for showing me that our wounds do not define us. I love you.

Dad, you have a whole page, so wait for it. . . .

Susan and Gary Hoover, the most eloquent words could never sum up how much you mean to me. I love you and thank God that you are my family. Your constant love, support, wisdom, and kindness is a gift straight from Him.

Keitha Miller, my favorite sister in the world! Thank you for how you support me, forgive me, and still love me when I'm that overbearing older sister. I couldn't ask for a better sister; you are it!

Katelyn Bailey and Elina Riccardelli, thank you for playing with my kiddos so I could write! You two have been a gift to our family, and we are so grateful for you. We love you!

Sally Clarkson, what can I even say? No words could ever do justice to how you have impacted my life. You are pure grace to me. Thank you for how you have invested in me, loved me, and taught me to persevere, hold onto my ideals, and live by faith. You have been the wind in my sails.

Jan Long Harris, thank you for your patience and grace through the crazy-long journey of getting this book out to the world. You have been so kind and such a gift to me. I hope to work with you for years to come.

Bonne Steffen, thank you for helping me not look like an idiot in this book! *Anvils*. I can't believe I had that in there. You have been such a blessing to me. Thank you for your time, hard work, patience, and for making me a better writer.

To the rest of the Tyndale team: Nancy Clausen, Sarah Atkinson, Jillian VandeWege, Katie Dodillet, and Cassidy Gage, you all have been wonderful, and I am grateful to each of you. I have so enjoyed getting to know you, and I pray I have the honor of working with all of you again.

Bill Jensen, thank you for being there for me when I needed someone who knew the ropes. You have been an incredible gift to me with your knowledge, your listening ear, and your friendship.

Logan Wolfram, my dearest friend, your prayers and support have meant the world to me. You are my sister, my kindred, my mimi. Thank you for being there for me.

Denise Hughes, thank you for teaching me about what good writing really is and for speaking truth to me about discipline. Thank you for telling me that God didn't call me to maintain things, but to birth things. That has forever changed me.

Crystal Paine, thank you for always supporting me and being a cheerleader for me. You are one of the most generous people I have ever met. You inspire me every day.

Amy Smoker, it is wild to me how God brought you into my life. You are such a gift to my family and me. Thank you for being normal! Thank you for potato soup, gingerbread cookies, being "the best" to my kids, as well as being my friend. You have been water to my dry bones.

Renee Behringer, Robyn Sowada, and Robin Troyer, thank you so much for praying me through this book! I am convinced it was your prayers that got me through. I am grateful to each of you.

Sarah Zurin, thank you for your grace and your prayers for me. I love you, sister.

Lynn Hamer, thank you for being such a support to me as you've watched me in the crazy times trying to write and still maintain my life! You have always been grace to me, and I'm thankful for our friendship.

Ginny Walls, thank you for your friendship, your wisdom, and the time you have spent caring for my family and reading over my manuscripts. You are so dear to me.

Choosing How to Live Gals, you all are the best! Even through the starts and stops, you have stuck around and made this book better. Thank you for your time, your feedback, your encouragement, and your friendship. Grateful to each one of you!

Sherri Graham and the Hilton Hotel, thank you for being awesome! I have loved working with you all, and I am grateful for the quiet, beautiful rooms I've had to write in. I love it there! And Sherri, you are beautiful and dear. Thank you for your friendship.

Liz and Ben Ehrhart from Furnace Hills B&B, thank you for making my dream come true of writing in a cabin in the woods with a fire and a dog. I adore your B&B and will be back!

Mason Currey, thank you for your book *Daily Rituals: How Artists Work* because it so inspired me.

Ernest Hemingway (because you're one of my favorites, even though I hear it will only end badly for me).

FOR MY DAD

WHEN I WROTE my first book, *Desperate: Hope for the Mom Who Needs to Breathe*, I left out a very important person in my acknowledgments. I'd like to remedy that right now.

Robert Clark, Dad, thank you for always making me feel loved; there has never been a minute of my life where I felt unloved by you. You have always hung the moon in my world, and you are my hero. From the nights of reading *The Baby-Sitters Club*, to the tears in your eyes when I'd fly to see my mom, to Christmas nights where we'd eat wings and watch James Bond movies, you saying nightly, "Sleep tight, don't let the bedbugs bite. I love you, and I'll see you in the morning," to your "Clean up your room" notes (which always cracked me up!), to long hugs, a 20th Players birthday surprise, flaming pink flamingos when I was sick, boxes full of candy, Billy Joel's "Uptown Girl," Swedish Fish in the ears, Madonna and the microphone at the dealership, gentleness, flame shoes . . .

I pray my children feel and know the love I have for them as deeply as the way I felt it from you.

I love you, Dad. Thank you for giving me the security of love. In the words of Bette, *you are the wind beneath my wings.*

GROUP DISCUSSION GUIDE

THIS DISCUSSION GUIDE is designed for a group study of *Longing for Paris*. The questions are arranged by chapter so that you may adjust for a shorter or longer study, as best fits your needs. Feel free to focus on the questions or issues that resonate most with your group. The guide is intended as a basis for deeper conversation, community, and spiritual growth, so use it as a starting point, and let God guide your time together.

AUTHOR'S NOTE

- Do you ever feel like you can't catch up with your life? What are some areas in which you wish you could use a pause button? What areas do you struggle with most when it comes to self-discipline?
- Are there pieces of your soul you feel you've hidden away since having children? What are they? Did you snuff them out because you felt they were selfish, or did they just sort of fall away in the busyness of life?

- Sarah Mae longs for Paris, but what she's really longing for is something deeper, the root of something else. What is something you long for? Do you think there's a deeper root to the longing? If so, what do you think it is?
- Do you feel free to enjoy your life? Why or why not?

INTRODUCTION: THE CATALYST

- Sarah Mae sometimes daydreams about having two lives, one where she is doing exactly what she's doing now, and one where she is in Paris as a full-time writer. If you had a second life, where would you spend it, and what would you be doing?
- Do you ever struggle with the tension between your longings and your reality? How do you deal with the tension? Do you stuff it away or find ways to reconcile it?
- Do you believe certain longings in our souls are designed by God? If so, what might they be designed to lead us toward? How can we tell the difference between God-inspired dreams and desires that might not be from Him?

CHAPTER ONE: UNTANGLING MY SOUL

- Have you ever wrestled with God over how He views you as a woman or how He views women in general? Looking at the life of Jesus, what do we see in His interactions with women that reveal God's heart towards us?
- Has there been a specific time in your spiritual walk when you've "seen" God—when your eyes have been opened to the truth of His love and kindness? What were

the circumstances? If not, or if you are desperate to hear Him now, why does Sarah Mae call you blessed? Do you believe God hears you and cares for you?

- Do you believe God cares about your dreams? Why or why not?
- Do you believe you can live a cross-centered life and still be happy? *Happy* is an unpopular word in the Christian vernacular; why do you think that is? Do you think God is ever happy?
- If your dreams never came to fruition the way you've longed for them to, is it still settled in your heart that God is good? Why or why not?

CHAPTER TWO: EVERYDAY ADVENTURE

- Adventure, to Sarah Mae, doesn't mean bungee jumping or skydiving. What about you? What's the craziest adventure you've ever had? What's one you still dream of having? Name something others might consider adventurous that you would never, ever want to do.
- Do you and your family take adventures together? If so, what do you do? If not, what might be getting in the way? What's something adventurous you could do right at home, and what would it take to make it happen in the weeks before this study concludes?
- Sarah Mae shares the story of a mom who turned a simple fast-food stop into a cherished memory of adventure. What is an adventure that thrilled you as a child? What made it so special to you?

- Have you ever done an act of service that took you outside your comfort zone? What was it, and how did it turn out?
- At one point, Jesse struggled with resentment toward God, who seemed to "put a dream in his heart [but] then gave him a disability that would prevent that dream from ever coming true." Do you or does anyone you know struggle with a similar situation? How has that affected your relationship with God? How do you get through it?

CHAPTER THREE: LEARNING TO SAVOR

- What's the most special and memorable meal you've ever eaten? Can you think of some instances in the Bible when people shared a meal together? What do you think it is about food that creates memories and brings people together?
- Have you ever done the Daniel Diet Sarah Mae describes or any specialized eating plan? If so, what was the experience like for you? How does paying attention to what we eat teach us about our habits, hearts, and bodies?
- Sarah Mae decides to cook more and become more hospitable as a result of her "Paris experiment" in savoring her food. Do you feel like you are savoring your experiences and your life? If not, how might you start to do so?

CHAPTER FOUR: BEAUTY

- What do you think makes a woman beautiful? Who's someone in your own circle of friends who exemplifies those qualities? Could you give her a call today to let her know you see and admire the beauty within her?

- What is keeping you from a deeper relationship with the Lord? How can you pursue God's face more intentionally this week?
- Have you ever done a media fast like the one Sarah Mae describes in this chapter? If so, what was the experience like? If not, would you like to do one? Consider setting aside a day or even a few hours to try this experiment and see how God speaks to you in the silence of your attention.
- What is one of your biggest distractions, and how much time does it take away from how you really want to live? How could you take that time and use it fruitfully to pursue your dreams and longings instead?
- Where is a place you could go this week to experience beauty?

CHAPTER FIVE: A NEW DEFINITION OF ROMANCE

- What would your ideal romantic date look like?
- After reading about Sarah Mae's new perspective of how she views romance, can you think of ways your spouse or partner has been "practically" romantic toward you in your everyday lives?
- What do you do when you feel as if you can't go on in a relationship any longer? Who do you call for help and support? What do you say to God? What Scriptures do you rely on?

- What does Sarah Mae mean by saying "Paris is in the details"? Do you agree? Where do you see Paris in the details of your own life?

CHAPTER SIX: THE WONDER OF IT ALL (STRIVING TO MOTHER WELL)

- Sarah Mae's kids know that she has a thing for Paris. Do your kids know about your dreams? Why might it be valuable for them to know this part of you, and how could you teach them about it?
- How can you teach your children about the beauty in the world? How might you equip them to be people of light and inspire them to pursue their potential? Would that look different for each of your children depending on their personalities? How so?
- What is your biggest dream for your children? For yourself as a mother? What will it take for you to look back at the end of your days and feel confident that you lived well?
- What does nurturing your children's souls mean to you? What about nurturing your own soul? Do you sometimes feel you have to choose between one or the other? How do you react to that tension?

CHAPTER SEVEN: HOLY DNA

- How would you answer the question Sarah Mae is asked in this chapter: What would you do if Jesus walked into the room right now? List some of the ways in which people in the Bible reacted when they encountered Jesus.

- Sarah Mae says "French women are known for accepting who they are, embracing it, and working to grow into it. They don't strive to be like someone else; they want to be fully themselves." In what areas of your life do you feel confident and assured? In what areas do you still struggle with insecurity?
- Sarah Mae thanks God for the ability and freedom to make choices. What have you been afraid to choose in your own life for fear of failure? If you could make one life-change choice right now that would bring more joy to yourself and/or your family, what would it be?
- What are some of the ways your own longing heart can be used for good or bad? How might your longings be pointing you (or be used to point others) to God?
- Take a few moments to list your dreams. Which ones are for this season, and which ones are not? How can you tell the difference?

CHAPTER EIGHT: CALLED TO SPARKLE

- How has God wooed you? What's your story?
- What brokenness has God allowed you to experience so that His light can shine through?
- "God always seems to bring things back until we deal with them," Sarah Mae reflects. Has this been your own experience? Is there something you haven't dealt with that keeps coming up? How can you begin to deal with whatever that is?
- Look around you. What areas of need do you see in your

family, in your friends' lives, in your church, or in your community where you have the capacity to serve and be a light?

CHAPTER 9: HOME

- How does knowing that all of our longings ultimately point to God, His beauty, and our heavenly home help you as you walk out this earthy life? Have you had any shifts in perspective?
- Sarah Mae describes a book that made her long for heaven. Have you ever read a book or a passage of Scripture or had an experience that affected you in that way? What was it?
- What can you learn from the dreams of your heart about your own longing for heaven?
- Why does Sarah Mae say she hesitates to fully invest in her earthly home? How do you think God wants us to dwell in our homes here on earth?
- What has the message of *Longing for Paris* inspired you to do with regard to your own dreams, longings, contentment, and everyday adventures?
- If you could ask Sarah Mae one question, what would it be? Tweet her @sarahmae and use hashtag #LongingForParis. She'll do her best to answer your questions!

ABOUT THE AUTHOR

SARAH MAE is a writer who encourages women to *keep on* and *begin again*. She is a wife, mom, homeschool teacher, conference founder, speaker, and piecrust botcher.

She makes her home in the beautiful Amish countryside of Pennsylvania, where she often ponders what life would be like if she actually *finished* all the laundry.

You can find her at sarahmae.com.

NOTES

1. Julia Child, *My Life in France* (New York: Alfred A. Knopf, 2006), 18.
2. Mireille Guiliano, *French Women Don't Get Fat* (New York: Alfred A. Knopf, 2005), 206–207.
3. Debra Ollivier, *Entre Nous* (New York: St. Martin's Press, 2003), 3–4.
4. John Piper, "What Does It Mean to Seek the Lord?" *Desiring God* (blog), August 19, 2009, http://www.desiringgod.org/blog/posts/what-does -it-mean-to-seek-the-lord.
5. A. W. Tozer, *Life in the Spirit* (Peabody, MA: Hendrickson Publishing, 2009), 143–144.
6. Richard Foster, *Celebration of Discipline* (San Francisco: HarperSanFrancisco, 2002), 17.
7. Robert Robinson, "Come Thou Fount of Every Blessing," 1758.
8. A. W. Tozer, *The Set of the Sail* (Camp Hill, PA: Wingspread Publishers, 2010), 130–132.
9. A. W. Tozer, *The Crucified Life* (Grand Rapids, MI: Bethany House, 2011), 152.
10. A. W. Tozer, *The Pursuit of God* (Harrisburg, PA: Christian Publications, 1948), 34, 39.
11. As found in William J. Bennett, *The Book of Virtues* (New York: Simon & Schuster, 1993), 134.
12. We found a free one at http://www.5lovelanguages.com/profile/children/.
13. M. Scott Peck, *The Road Less Traveled* (New York: Touchstone, 2003), 23.
14. Clay Clarkson, *Heartfelt Discipline* (Monument, CO: Whole Heart Press, 2014), 25.

15. "Media and Children," *American Academy of Pediatrics*, accessed March 20, 2015, http://www.aap.org/en-us/advocacy-and-policy/aap-health -initiatives/Pages/Media-and-Children.aspx.

16. David L. Hill, "Why to Avoid TV Before Age 2," last modified May 11, 2013, http://www.healthychildren.org/English/family-life/Media/Pages /Why-to-Avoid-TV-Before-Age-2.aspx.

17. Sally Clarkson, "Killing the Soul of Children—Revisited," *Sally Clarkson* (blog), March 27, 2013, http://sallyclarkson.com/killing-the-soul-of -children-revisited-2/.

18. John Yates and Susan Alexander Yates, *Raising Kids with Character That Lasts* (Grand Rapids, MI: Revell, 2011), 232.

19. John Lynch, "Truefaced Two Roads Message," accessed March 20, 2015, https://www.youtube.com/watch?v=Rfy03PEVUhQ.

20. Joel N. Clark, *Awake* (Grand Rapids: Zondervan, 2012), 173.

21. John Eldredge, *The Journey of Desire* (Nashville: Thomas Nelson, 2000), 167.

22. Ibid., 168.

23. Ibid., 181.

24. This is a slightly adapted version of my original March 8, 2012, blog post "My Abortion Story," which you can find at sarahmae.com/abortion.

25. Linda Cochrane, *Forgiven and Set Free* (Grand Rapids: Baker Books, 1999).

26. This story is adapted from: September McCarthy, "How God Led Me to Stop. . . ," *One September Day* (blog), November 4, 2010, http://www .septembermccarthy.com/2010/11/how-god-led-me-to-stop/.

27. Mark Buchanan, *Things Unseen* (Colorado Springs: WaterBrook Multnomah, 2006), 136.

28. Leif Enger, *Peace Like a River* (New York: Grove Press, 2001), 300–301.

29. Inspired by Sara Groves's song, "What Do I Know?"

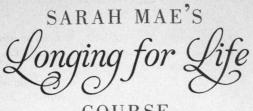

SARAH MAE'S
Longing for Life
COURSE

You've read *Longing for Paris*, and it opened wide something in you that has been waiting to be released. You want to enjoy your life. You want to delight. You want to be a part of this beautiful Kingdom bearing that you are called into. *You want to live.*

But how? How can you live well when you feel like you can't even get your life together in order to *begin*?

Friend, this course is for you—the woman who has desires and longings but just needs some guidance and step-by-step help.

Join Sarah Mae in this multisession intensive companion course designed to help you craft the unregrettable life you're longing for.

You *can* begin, but you don't have to go at it alone.

LEARN MORE AND SEE COURSE TOPICS, DESCRIPTIONS, AND SAMPLE VIDEOS BY VISITING **WWW.LONGINGFORLIFE.COM** OR SCANNING THE QR CODE BELOW!

For those who have ever whispered
"I just can't be a mom today . . ."

desperate

HOPE *for the* MOM

Who Needs to Breathe

SARAH MAE & SALLY CLARKSON

"I hold these pages, words of Sarah Mae's and Sally's, that are a gift to every mother, that welcome mothers everywhere out of hiding and loneliness and into a fellowship of sisters and mentors, that will make you feel not alone, that will make you feel there is real God-given hope."

—Ann Voskamp, *New York Times* bestselling author of *One Thousand Gifts*

FIND OUT MORE AT DESPERATEMOM.COM.

WWW.THOMASNELSON.COM

CP0946

*Live courageously, increase your faith,
and become a person of influence.*

IT'S TIME TO OWN YOUR LIFE.

Foreword by Sarah Mae, Angela Perritt & Ruth Schwenk

own
your
life

*Living with deep intention, bold faith,
and generous love*

SALLY CLARKSON

Join Sally Clarkson on a journey to live each day
with spiritual intention—and experience the breathtaking story that God has in store for you. As
you begin to own your life, you'll come alive with
confidence, energy, and purpose as you discover
His fingerprints in your most ordinary days.

Find out more at **SallyClarkson.com**.